Outstanding Dissertations in

ECONOMICS

A Continuing Garland Research Series

Four Essays in the Theory of Uncertainty and Portfolio Choice

Jonathan Eaton

Garland Publishing, Inc.
New York & London, 1979

Library of Congress Cataloging in Publication Data

Eaton, Jonathan, 1950–
Four essays in the theory of uncertainty and portfolio choice.

(Outstanding dissertations in economics)
Originally presented as the author's thesis, Yale, 1976.
Bibliography: p.
1. Uncertainty—Mathematical models.
2. Investments—Mathematical models. 3. Saving and investment—Mathematical models.
4. Economics—Mathematical models. I. Title.
II. Series.
HB615.E27 1979 330'.01'51 78-75071
ISBN 0-8240-4145-3

All volumes in this series are printed on acid-free, 250-year-life paper.

Printed in the United States of America.

INTRODUCTION TO THE 1979 EDITION

In the three years since this thesis was submitted a considerable amount of research has appeared on the problems that it considers. It is interesting at this point to examine how the thesis relates to what has gone on since, both to see what light it may shed on current discussions and to examine its analysis and conclusions in light of the technical progress that has occurred in the intervening time.

The discussion surrounding the "New International Economic Order," specifically on the design and operation of the proposed integrated commodity program (see Secretary-General of UNCTAD, [1975]), has focussed attention on commodity price variability and on the effects of price stabilization schemes, problems considered in the first three essays. While some of what has been written since has examined price stabilization schemes in a more general equilibrium context the conclusion that stabilization schemes can reduce economic welfare remains intact. Newbery and Stiglitz [1979] have considered the effects of price stabilization schemes in a number of contexts with this result. An important conclusion of their analysis is that the effects of uncertainty on resource allocation are themselves important in determining whether or not price stability is desirable. For example, price instability which is negatively correlated with output instability can actually reduce income uncertainty for producers. A price stabilization scheme may thus reduce average output by increasing the riskiness of some undertakings. A point made in the second essay is that an examination of areas under a demand curve cannot adequately demonstrate the effects of price uncertainty on consumer welfare. An implication of the Newbery-Stiglitz analysis is that the supply curve is equally inadequate in illustrating the effects of instability on supply. Changes in the distribution of price will affect the position of the curve itself. Newbery and Stiglitz consider situations in which all resource allocation must occur *ex ante*.

An implication of the analysis in the first three essays is that introducing ex post mobility of productive resources will detract from the desirability of a price stabilization scheme, reinforcing the point that stabilization can reduce welfare.

Two developments of a more technical nature should be pointed out. First, Townsend [1977] shows that a price stabilization scheme which fixes price at a level at which expected excess demand is zero (or at any other level, for that matter) cannot be sustained indefinitely. Such a scheme will deplete any buffer stock of finite size in finite time with probability one. Thus the stabilization scheme discussed in Part III of the first essay cannot be maintained forever. The point that such a scheme might be undesirable even if it were feasible remains, and continues to suggest that many feasible schemes might reduce welfare.

Secondly, Flemming, Turnovsky and Kemp [1977] have criticized the use of the arithmetic-mean preserving spread as a characterization of increased uncertainty in the distribution of a relative price. An increase in price uncertainty which preserves the arithmetic mean of a relative price under one choice of numeraire does not preserve the arithmetic mean under another choice. They propose, instead, a characterization of increased uncertainty as a spread which preserves the geometric mean of the price as the geometric mean is insensitive to the numeraire choice. I have examined the effects of geometric-mean preserving spreads in relative prices on expected utility and on the optimal savings of a consumer in subsequent research (see Eaton, [1978a]) While this treatment of the problem yields conditions which are symmetric in commodities, the ambiguities pointed out in the effects of uncertainty on utility and savings in the second essay remain as does the intuition behind these ambiguities. I have also examined the effects on welfare and resource allocation of a geometric-mean preserving spread in the terms of trade of a small country (see Eaton, [1979]). Again, the intuition developed in the examination of trade and uncertainty in the third essay remains for the most part intact.

The fourth essay, dealing with the effects of uncertainty in production on a growing economy, provides a model in which the effects of taxation on risk taking can be examined in general equilibrium. The model presented in Part III of this essay has been extended to examine this issue extensively (see Eaton, [1978b]) and has spurred an interest in the effects of taxation on behavior under uncertainty and on the design of efficient tax systems in a stochastic environment. Eaton and Rosen [1979a and 1979b] report on some recent research in this area.

While a considerable amount of research on the economic problems arising from uncertainty and imperfect information has now been done there remain many areas of economics where the implications of uncertainty have not been explored. Past research has shown that introducing considerations of risk and imperfect information can overturn in rather surprising ways results derived from the analysis of deterministic models. I expect that the analysis of the economics of uncertainty will remain one of the most exciting areas of research in economics for many years to come.

Princeton, New Jersey

July 1979

REFERENCES

Eaton, J., [1978a] "Price Variability, Utility and Savings" Econometric Research Program Research Memorandum No. 227, Princeton University

Eaton, J. [1978b] Fiscal Policy, Inflation and the Accumulation of Risky Capital Econometric Research Program Research Memorandum No. 226, Princeton University

Eaton, J., [1979] "The Allocation of Resources in an Open Economy with Uncertain Terms of Trade" International Economic Review, 20 (forthcoming)

Eaton, J. and H. S. Rosen [1979a] "Taxation, Human Capital, and Uncertainty" Industrial Relations Section Working Paper #117, Princeton University

Eaton, J. and H.S. Rosen [1979b] "Notes on Optimal Wage Taxation and Uncertainty" mimeo, Princeton University

Flemming, J.S., S.J. Turnovsky and M.C. Kemp [1977] "On the Choice of Numeraire and Certainty Price in General Equilibrium Models of Price Uncertainty," Review of Economic Studies, 64(3), pp. 573-584

Newbery, D. and J.E. Stiglitz [1979] The Economic Impact of Price Stabilization, Oxford University Press, forthcoming

Secretary-General of UNCTAD [1975] "An Integrated Programme for Commodities: Specific Proposals for Decision and Action by Governments" Report TD/B/C.1/193

Townsend, R.M., [1977] "The Eventual Failure of Price Fixing Schemes." Journal of Economic Theory, 14 pp. 190-199

FOUR ESSAYS IN THE THEORY OF UNCERTAINTY AND PORTFOLIO CHOICE

A Dissertation

Presented to the Faculty of the Graduate School

of

Yale University

in Candidacy for the Degree of

Doctor of Philosophy

by

Jonathan Eaton

1976

ABSTRACT

FOUR ESSAYS IN THE THEORY OF UNCERTAINTY AND PORTFOLIO CHOICE

Jonathan Eaton

Yale University 1976

This thesis is concerned with the effect of uncertainty on welfare, on the optimal value of control variables and on equilibrium. A general model of optimization under uncertainty is developed in the first essay. It is shown that increased uncertainty in a parameter of a strictly concave objective function need not reduce its expected value when there are control variables which may be set after the actual value of the stochastic parameter is known. This model is then used to demonstrate that increased technological uncertainty does not necessarily reduce expected welfare when production decisions occur after technological parameters are known. The welfare effects of a price stabilization program under alternative assumptions about production flexibility are then examined.

The second essay considers the effect of increased relative price uncertainty on expected utility and on optimal savings behavior of the household. It is demonstrated that the effect on either is ambiguous and depends on the elasticity of substitution in utility and on attitudes toward risk.

A model to consider the effects of uncertainty in the terms of trade and technology on the expected welfare, optimal specialization and optimal reserve holdings of a small trading nation is developed in the third essay. In the first part, it is demonstrated that expected welfare is more likely to rise and optimal reserve levels more likely to fall in response to increased uncertainty when production and consumption allocations may be modified in response to actual outcomes. The second part of this essay introduces productive capital into the model and considers optimal investment under uncertainty. It is shown that price uncertainty may lead to diversification of investment even if investment would be completely specialized under certainty and if preferences are characterized by neutrality toward risk.

A stochastic model of money and growth is developed in the first part of the fourth essay. Uncertainty in the rate of depreciation or in the production function is shown to raise the output-capital ratio when savings and portfolio allocation decisions are interest inelastic. The effect of increased savings, increased demand for money and increased government expenditure on the expected output-capital ratio in steady state is shown to be ambiguous, in contrast with the results for the deterministic case. A model embodying interest and inflation responsive savings and portfolio behavior is developed in the second part of this essay. The effects of alternative expenditure and tax policies on the equilibrium capital-labor ratio and rate of inflation are derived.

In memory of my father and to my mother

ACKNOWLEDGMENTS

I am indebted to the members of my dissertation committee, James Tobin, James L. McCabe and Gary Smith for their invaluable suggestions, criticisms and support throughout the progress of this thesis. I am also grateful to Donald J. Brown, David S. Sibley and Ward Whitt for their extremely useful comments. All responsibility for remaining error lies, of course, with the author.

Mrs. Glena Ames has prepared the final manuscript from my barely legible drafts with enormous accuracy and patience. To her I owe a large debt of thanks.

I gratefully acknowledge the financial support of the National Science Foundation and Yale University during my years as a graduate student.

TABLE OF CONTENTS

TABLE OF CONTENTS, continued

TABLE OF CONTENTS, continued

INTRODUCTION

A major concern of economic theorists in the last decade has been the integration of problems of costly information and uncertainty into the theoretical frameworks developed for deterministic situations in which information is costless. Questions of two general types arise when uncertainty about future outcomes is introduced into an economic model: First, what is the effect of uncertainty of different types on economic welfare? Second, how does the introduction of uncertainty affect the optimal values of control variables which must be set before outcomes are known? These considerations suggest a further question which is the effect of information about uncertain future outcomes on welfare.

This thesis is concerned with questions of these types in four contexts: (1) the effect of increased uncertainty in technology on welfare and optimal production in a two-sector closed economy; (2) the effect of future relative price uncertainty on welfare and on the optimal savings-consumption and portfolio-allocation decisions of the household; (3) the effect of uncertainty about the prices of traded goods and technology on national welfare and on optimal foreign reserve holdings and structure of investment in a small open economy; and (4) the effect of introducing uncertainty in production on the steady state of a growing monetary economy.

The first area of economics in which uncertainty has played a central role is quite naturally the analysis of insurance and gambling. Mathematical models of behavior toward risk originate with Bernoulli in the seventeenth century [1953]. Modern analysis of insurance originates with the work of Ramsey [1931] and the axioms of von Neumann and Morgenstern [1953]. Since their seminal work the major contributor to the area is no doubt Arrow [1971].[1]

Formally incorporating the purchase of insurance, either in the form of contingent commodities as in the treatment by Debreu [1959] or as securities as in Arrow's analysis [1971], into the general equilibrium Walrasian framework has proven very simple. With suitable redefinition the economic theory designed for analysis of deterministic situations can be extended to situations of uncertainty as long as there is no constraint on the number of markets operating at any moment.

Radner [1968] among others has criticized this approach as unrealistic in ignoring transactions and information costs. When these are present a complete set of markets may not exist in which case a major property of the system is lost. It may no longer be possible for all trades to be agreed upon before information on the outcome of an uncertain state of nature is available. The addition of such information may create further opportunities for trade on "spot" markets. Anticipation of future trading opportunities on such markets generates a demand for wealth or liquidity or, more simply, goods to be traded for other goods on these markets at currently uncertain prices.

Interest in economic behavior under uncertainty has arisen from

---

[1] Current research in the area of insurance markets is being conducted by Wilson [1976].

a very different source in the post-war era. In reaction to the acceptance of the Keynesian model of income determination by a large number of economists neoclassicists criticized the framework of the General Theory for its lack of foundation in microeconomic theory. A number of postulates of the Keynesian theory were shown to be inconsistent with maximizing behavior on the part of rational economic agents in a deterministic environment.

In response to a criticism of the Keynesian theory of liquidity preference by Leontief [1947], Tobin [1958] demonstrated that Keynes' formulation of the demand for money was consistent with maximization of expected utility in situations involving risk. The analysis stimulated subsequent research into the theory of portfolio choice. Its implications for financial model building have been recognized and the theory of portfolio choice now represents a major component of post-Keynesian macroeconomic theory.

Since Tobin's contribution a large amount of the research into the economics of behavior under uncertainty has been motivated by a desire to reconcile the Keynesian macroeconomic framework with Walrasian microeconomic theory. The volume edited by Phelps [1970] contains several analyses in which unemployment equilibrium is attributed to uncertainty and imperfect information on wages in alternative labor markets. According to this viewpoint unemployment may be interpreted as search activity or the production of information. More recently Iwai [1974] has derived a microeconomic theory of the Phillips curve based on individual firms' uncertainty about their product demand and factor supply curves. Another contribution has been Sibley's [1975] analysis of the theory of the consumption function in terms of optimal behavior in response to uncertainty about future labor income.

A number of economists have developed Walrasian models modified along the lines suggested by Radner's criticisms which generate Keynesian equilibria. Notable in this group are Hahn [1965] and Grandmont and Laroque [1976]. Uncertainty plays a major role in these analyses.

While macroeconomics has provided a major impetus to research in the area a number of other fields have suggested problems related to uncertainty. Brainard [1967] has shown that uncertainty **about** the responsiveness of target variables to policy instruments modifies optimal policies. The optimal response of specialization patterns to uncertainty in the terms of trade has been analyzed under different assumptions by Brainard and Cooper [1968], Batra [1975], Batra and Russell [1974] and Turnovsky [1974], among others. The effect of export-revenue uncertainty on optimal reserve policy is considered by McCabe and Sibley [1975] and Nsouli [1975]. Recent work by Spence [1974] has generated interest in the economics of market signalling. Stiglitz [1975] has suggested that the economics of uncertainty can provide a basis for a theory of hierarchies.

The economic situation in the earlier part of this decade generated my own interest in pursuing work in this area. The increased monopoly power of the Organization of Petroleum Exporting Countries generated enormous uncertainty about the future price of oil. The ability of the cartel to maintain high prices and the response of importing countries were unknown. The effect was both increased uncertainty about the terms of trade of the industrial countries and the relative prices facing consumers. I felt that the impact of uncertainty of this type on welfare, on aggregate demand and on optimal commercial, reserve and investment policy was inadequately understood.

More recently the instability of many commodity prices has led to proposals of world-wide price stabilization programs. Again I felt that the implications of these programs for aggregate demand, for optimal commercial, reserve and investment policy, and for the economic welfare of both individual nations and the world were inadequately understood.

These aspects of the contemporary situation motivated the analysis in the first three essays of the thesis. My interest in the treatment in the fourth essay was generated by a desire to understand the effects of uncertain aggregate supply and government policy toward risk in a dynamic general-equilibrium context. Previous work in the area has produced very meager results in terms of comparative steady-state analysis and no prescriptions for economic policy. Domar and Musgrave [1944] and Stiglitz [1969] have considered the effects of taxation on risk taking by individuals. The partial equilibrium nature of their analysis prevents them from tracing the risk absorbed by taxation to the consequent uncertainty in some other area of the economy. Unless government expenditure varies in harmony with the rate of return on the risky asset the uncertainty remains in disposable income, either as uncertainty in some other tax payment or in the rate of return on government debt. When the sources of uncertainty are many and small they will cancel out. When the uncertainty derives from such factors as economywide weather or political conditions, however, the entirety of policy response is critically important to considerations of investment and risk taking.

The thesis is divided into four essays. This format was chosen over the more usual one of chapter divisions since the analysis of each essay is relatively self-contained and deals with a quite distinct body of material. The qualitative effects of increased uncertainty on welfare and on optimizing behavior are, however, a question of concern throughout.

Much of the analysis considers the effects of "mean-preserving spreads" as defined by Hadar and Russell [1969] and Rothschild and Stiglitz [1970] in the subjective probability distribution functions of unknown parameters on welfare and on optimal values of control variables. In continuous-time analysis increased uncertainty is represented as an increase in the coefficient of the random component of the diffusion process describing the motion of the random variable in question. Throughout the thesis it is assumed that agents behave according to the von Neumann-Morgenstern [1953] axioms to maximize the expected value of their objective functions.

The first essay develops a general framework for optimization under uncertainty. In the first section of this essay theorems on the effects of increased uncertainty on the expected value of the objective function, on the value of information, and on optimal values of control variables are presented. These theorems are applied extensively in the following two essays. One of them demonstrates that even when the objective function is concave in the random variable increased uncertainty will not necessarily reduce the expected value of the objective function when there are control variables which may be set once knowledge of the outcome of the random process is available.

The second section of the first essay applies the framework developed in the first section to consider the effects of increased uncertainty in the transformation surface on welfare, optimal resource allocation and the value of information about parameters of the technology. It is shown that increased technological uncertainty may raise expected utility. The welfare effects of a price stabilization policy in the context of this model are derived.

The effects of increased price uncertainty on the expected utility and on the optimal savings of an individual consumer are treated in the second essay. Waugh [1944] and Samuelson [1972] have shown that relative price instability increases the expected utility of a consumer whose utility function is characterized by constant marginal utility of either income or the composite of all other commodities. In this essay it is shown that when the return on savings is uncorrelated with the price in question the welfare effect of increased relative price uncertainty is generally ambiguous. It is more likely to be positive, however, the greater the income-compensated price elasticity of demand for the commodity whose price is becoming more uncertain relative to the degree of relative risk aversion and the share of purchases of the commodity in total expenditure. When there is an available asset whose rate of return is perfectly correlated with the price in question increased price uncertainty always raises the expected value of utility.

The effects of non-wealth-income and interest-rate uncertainty on optimal savings have been treated by a number of authors.[2] Their analyses take place in a one-commodity context in which only variation in real income is introduced. In the second essay the effect of increased

[2]Among them are Phelps [1962], Mirrlees [1965], Leland [1968], Levhari and Srinivasan [1969], Hahn [1970], Sandmo [1970], Rothschild and Stiglitz [1971], Mirman [1971] and Merton [1971].

relative price uncertainty in a future period on current savings is considered. It is shown that for consumers whose utility functions are characterized by constant relative risk aversion increased relative price uncertainty increases savings both for those with degree of relative risk aversion less than one and for those with very high degrees of relative risk aversion. At intermediate levels the effect of increased price uncertainty on savings may be negative. Increased relative price uncertainty increases expected utility in future periods for the less risk averse. For this group a given amount of savings will yield greater utility when price uncertainty increases. Increased price uncertainty is therefore like an increase in the interest rate for consumers with low or moderate degrees of relative risk aversion. Consequently their consumption will increase or decrease as their degree of relative risk aversion exceeds or is exceeded by one. For the very risk averse the income effect of increased price uncertainty lowers expected future utility. This generates a demand for higher savings.

The effect of uncertainty in the terms of trade and in the technology of a small trading country on national welfare, optimal specialization and reserve holding is treated in the third essay. It is shown in the first section of this essay that when the allocation of resources for production and consumption must precede knowledge of actual prices and technological relationships increased uncertainty in the terms of trade necessarily reduces expected national welfare and increases optimal holdings of foreign reserves. Increased uncertainty in the terms of trade reduces optimal specialization while increased technological uncertainty reduces optimal production of the commodity with uncertain technology. If the allocation of resources for consumption but not production may occur with knowledge of actual technological relationships these results are unaffected. When consumption decisions take place with knowledge of the realized terms of trade, however, the effect of increased price uncertainty on expected welfare, optimal reserve holdings and optimal specialization becomes ambiguous. When both the allocation of resources for production as well as consumption may occur after price and technological outcomes are known then increased uncertainty of either kind has an ambiguous effect. Reversals are more likely the greater the elasticities of substitution in production and consumption.

The second section of the third essay introduces considerations of optimal investment in the context of uncertain terms of trade. It is assumed that capital is immobile between sectors while labor is not. A first result of this section is that increased price uncertainty is more likely to increase expected welfare the higher labor productivity and the higher the elasticity of substitution between factors in each industry. A second result is that introducing price uncertainty increases optimal investment in the production of import substitutes but has an ambiguous effect on investment in exports. In either case increased investment increases the elasticity of substitution between sectors. Increased investment in exports increases exposure to risk in the terms of trade while increased investment in the import-substitute sector reduces this exposure. These two considerations reinforce each other in the case of investment in the production of import substitutes but work against each other for export investment. Thirdly, it is shown that even if national preferences are characterized by risk neutrality and the production transformation surface is linear optimal investment and production may not be completely specialized under uncertainty as they would be in the case of deterministic terms of trade.

The fourth essay, concerned with the long-run effects of monetary and fiscal policy in the presence of uncertainty in production and wealth effects in consumption, is more macroeconomic in focus. The first section of this essay demonstrates that introducing uncertainty in production, in contrast to uncertainty in the natural rate of growth considered in the stochastic growth models of Bourgignon [1974] and Merton [1975], reduces the expected capital-labor ratio. It is then shown for the deterministic case that introducing a consumption relationship with wealth effects can reverse many of the policy prescriptions of the long-run money and growth model. Finally a monetary growth model imbedding uncertain technology and a limited form of optimizing savings and portfolio behavior with wealth effects is developed.

The focus of these essays is primarily theoretical. There is no attempt to relate explicitly the conclusions of the analysis to contemporary economic problems. Nevertheless a few implications for current policy are worth stating.

First, policies which seek to reduce price uncertainty by stockpiling and reducing technological variability may reduce welfare or at least be inferior to policies which exploit variability by increasing information on future uncertain outcomes and increasing substitutability among outputs once outcomes are known. For instance, weather modification or irrigation to reduce rainfall variation or its effects on crop yields may represent an inferior policy to improved rainfall prediction and the planting of alternative crops most suited to the predicted rainfall.

Second, policies which increase the number and types of assets available to consumers reduce the adverse effects of relative price variation on consumer welfare. In economies in which price uncertainty is generated by exchange-rate variation, for example, consumers may be significantly better off when they can hold foreign exchange than when they cannot.

Third, the optimal response of policy to increased international price uncertainty may involve more than trade reduction. The apparent although as yet unperformed task of Project Independence has been the increased use of domestic energy sources to reduce oil imports. Trade reduction is an optimal response to increased price uncertainty when consumption and production must precede knowledge of price outcomes. The welfare loss from price uncertainty can also be reduced, however, by increasing the availability of information on future price movements and by increasing the short-run responsiveness of the economy to price changes. For example, a superior policy to replacing gasoline-burning by coal-burning power generation might be the development of a technology for which coal could be substituted for gasoline at short notice and at low cost. In general, optimal policy might involve investment in a more diverse set of technologies than if prices were certain.

Finally, policies which reduce the impact of variation in output on investment are desirable. The characteristics of the neoclassical production function imply that the productivity of a given average level of investment over a period will be greater when the investment has occurred smoothly rather than unevenly. When movements in income affect investment, while the expected marginal product of capital remains constant, expected output is lower than when investment is unaffected.

REFERENCES

Arrow, K. J. [1971] Essays in the Theory of Risk Bearing. Chicago: Markham.

Batra, R. N. [1975] The Pure Theory of International Trade under Uncertainty. London: Macmillan Press.

__________ and W. P. Russell [1974] "Gains from Trade under Uncertainty," American Economic Review, 64, pp. 1040-1048.

Bernoulli, D. [1953] "Exposition of a New Theory on the Measurement of Risk," translated by Louise Sommer, Econometrica, 22, pp. 175-192.

Bourgignon, F. [1974] "A Particular Class of Continuous-Time Stochastic Growth Models," Journal of Economic Theory, 9, pp. 141-158.

Brainard, W. C. [1967] "Uncertainty and the Effectiveness of Policy," American Economic Review, 57, pp. 411-425.

__________ and R. N. Cooper [1968] "Uncertainty and Diversification in International Trade," Studies in Agricultural Economics and Development, 8, Food Research Institute, Stanford University, pp. 257-285.

Domar, E. and R. Musgrave [1944] "Proportional Income Taxation and Risk Taking," Quarterly Journal of Economics, 56, pp. 388-422.

Debreu, G. [1959] Theory of Value. New York: Wiley.

Grandmont, J. M. and G. Laroque [1976] "On Temporary Keynesian Equilibria," Review of Economic Studies, 43(1), pp. 53-68.

Hadar, J. and W. Russell [1969] "Rules for Ordering Uncertain Prospects," American Economic Review, 59, pp. 25-34.

Hahn, F. H. [1970] "Savings under Uncertainty," Review of Economic Studies, 37, pp. 21-24.

__________ [1965] "On Some Problems of Proving the Existence of an Equilibrium in a monetary economy," The Theory of Interest Rates. Edited by F. H. Hahn and F. P. R. Brechling. London: Macmillan Publishers.

Iwai, K. [1974] "The Firm in Uncertain Markets and Its Price, Wage and Employment Adjustments," Review of Economic Studies, pp. 257-276.

Leland, H. E. [1968] "Savings and Uncertainty: The Precautionary Demand for Saving," Quarterly Journal of Economics, 82, pp. 465-473.

Leontief, W. [1947] "Postulates: Keynes General Theory and the Classicists," in The New Economics, edited by S. Harris. New York: Knopf.

Levhari, D. and T. N. Srinivasan [1969] "Optimal Savings under Uncertainty," Review of Economic Studies, 36, pp. 153-163.

McCabe, J. L. and D. S. Sibley [1975] "Optimal Foreign Debt Accumulation with Export Revenue Uncertainty," International Economic Review, (forthcoming).

Merton, R. C. [1971] "Optimum Consumption and Portfolio Rules in a Continuous-Time Model," Journal of Economic Theory, 3, pp. 373-413.

__________ [1975] "An Asymptotic Theory of Growth under Uncertainty," Review of Economic Studies, 42(3), pp. 375-394.

Mirman, L. J. [1971] "Uncertainty and Optimal Consumption Decisions," Econometrica, 39, pp. 179-185.

Mirrlees, J. A. [1965] "Optimal Accumulation under Uncertainty," unpublished manuscript, Cambridge, U.K., December.

Nsouli, S. M. [1975] "Theoretical Aspects of Trade Risk and Growth," Journal of International Economics, 5, pp. 239-253.

Phelps, E. S. [1962] "The Accumulation of Risky Capital: A Sequential Utility Analysis," Econometrica, 30, pp. 225-243.

__________ et al. [1970] Microeconomic Foundations of Employment and Inflation Theory. New York: Norton.

Radner, R. [1968] "Competitive Equilibrium under Uncertainty," Econometrica, 36, pp. 31-58.

Ramsey, F. P. [1931] "Truth and Probability" in The Foundations of Mathematics and Other Logical Essays. London: Kegan Paul, Trench and Trubner.

Rothschild, M. and J. E. Stiglitz [1970] "Increasing Risk: I. A Definition," Journal of Economic Theory, 2, pp. 225-243.

__________ [1971] "Increasing Risk: II. Its Economic Consequences," Journal of Economic Theory, 3, pp. 66-84.

Samuelson, P. A. [1972] "Feasible Price Stability," Quarterly Journal of Economics, 86, pp. 476-493.

Sandmo, A. [1970] "The Effect of Uncertainty on Saving Decisions," Review of Economic Studies, 37(1), pp. 353-360.

Sibley, D. S. [1975] "Permanent and Transitory Income Effects in a Model of Optimal Consumption with Wage Income Uncertainty," Journal of Economic Theory, 11, pp. 68-82.

Spence, A. M. [1974] Market Signalling. Cambridge: Harvard University Press.

Stiglitz, J. E. [1969] "The Effects of Wealth, Income and Capital Gains Taxation on Risk Taking," Quarterly Journal of Economics, 83, pp. 263-283.

__________ [1975] "Incentives, Risk and Information: Notes Toward a Theory of Hierarchy," Bell Journal of Economics, 6, pp. 552-579.

Tobin, J. [1958] "Liquidity Preference as Behavior Toward Risk," Review of Economic Studies, 25, pp. 65-86.

Turnovsky, S. J. [1974] "Technological and Price Uncertainty in a Ricardian Model of International Trade," Review of Economic Studies, 41, pp. 201-217.

von Neumann, J. and O. Morgenstern [1953] Theory of Games and Economic Behavior. Third Edition. New York: John Wiley.

Waugh, F. V. [1944] "Does the Consumer Benefit from Price Instability?" Quarterly Journal of Economics, 58, pp. 602-614.

Wilson, C. [1976] "A Model of Insurance Markets with Asymmetric Information," Cowles Foundation Discussion Paper No. 432, Yale University, New Haven.

ESSAY I

OPTIMIZATION UNDER UNCERTAINTY AND THE VALUE OF INFORMATION

I. Introduction

This essay presents some general results in the theory of optimization under uncertainty which are used extensively in the next two essays. The major concern of the entire thesis is the effect of increasing uncertainty on economic welfare and optimal behavior.

A natural way of defining increased uncertainty, discussed by Hadar and Russell [1969] is the replacement of the subjective probability function of a random variable $F(\theta)$ with another distribution $G(\theta)$ where the relationship of $G(\theta)$ to $F(\theta)$ is one of "second-order stochastic dominance." Rothschild and Stiglitz [1970] shows that a particular case of second-order stochastic dominance, the "mean-preserving spread," is equivalent to adding "white-noise" to a random variable, and that, for any concave function $U(\theta)$

$$(1.1) \qquad \int U(\theta)G'(\theta)d\theta \leq \int U(\theta)F'(\theta)d\theta$$

where $G(\theta)$ represents a mean-preserving spread in the distribution $F(\theta)$. It is this definition of increased uncertainty that is adopted in the present essay and in the two that follow.

Part II presents a rigorous definition of the mean-preserving spread and four results on the effects of increased uncertainty of this type. Theorem 1 derives a condition to determine the effect of increased uncertainty on the expected value of an objective function. A sufficient condition for the effect of increased uncertainty to increase the value of information is given in Theorem 2. Theorems 3 and 4 provide conditions for the effect of increased uncertainty on optimal values of controls which must be set prior to obtaining knowledge of the actual value of the random variable.

The theory of economic behavior under uncertainty is closely related to the economics of information. Arrow [1971] and Gould [1974] both provide definitions of the economic value of information. Part II presents a definition which represents a generalization of Gould's.

An application of some of the results of Part II is provided in Part III. A two-commodity general equilibrium model with uncertain production is developed. It is demonstrated that when the allocation of all resources in production must precede knowledge of the technological outcome convexity of preferences is sufficient for increased technological uncertainty to reduce expected welfare. If any allocation decision may follow knowledge of the actual outcome of the random variable increased technological uncertainty may increase expected utility even if the utility function is strictly concave.

Waugh [1944] and Oi [1961] demonstrate that increased relative price uncertainty will increase the expected utility of the risk-neutral consumer and increase the expected profits of a firm. In response to their arguments Samuelson [1972] points out that when there is no underlying uncertainty in technology or preferences then increased price uncertainty cannot increase social welfare. Samuelson's response leaves open the question of the relationship between social welfare and price uncertainty generated by technological uncertainty.

Part III shows that the relationship is generally ambiguous but may indeed be positive. If this is the case, stabilization programs do in fact reduce welfare.

II. Increased Uncertainty, Information and Control

We consider an agent who seeks to maximize the expected value of an objective function

(2.1) $$V(\alpha, \theta)$$

where α represents an n vector of control variables and θ a random variable with probability density function $f(\theta)$ of compact support. The values of the first k control variables are chosen before the outcome of the random process generating θ is known. These are referred to as *ex ante* controls. The remaining $n-k$ control variables are set with knowledge of θ and previously selected values of the *ex ante* control variables. These are defined as *ex post* controls.

The utility-maximizing values of the *ex post* controls satisfy the first-order conditions:

(2.2) $$V_{\alpha_i}(\alpha_a, \alpha_p, \theta) = 0 \ , \quad i = k+1, \ldots, n$$

where α_a represents the vector of the previously selected *ex ante* controls and α_p the vector of *ex post* control variables. If the conditions of the implicit function theorem are satisfied the system of equations (2.2) defines $n-k$ functions:

(2.3) $$\alpha_p^* = \alpha_p(\alpha_a, \theta) \ .$$

Assuming optimal selection of *ex post* controls allows the objective function (2.1) to be written as:

(2.4) $$V(\alpha_a, \alpha_p(\alpha_a, \theta), \theta) \equiv W(\alpha_a, \theta)$$

with expected value:

$$(2.5) \qquad \int W(\alpha_a,\ \theta)f(\theta)d\theta\ .$$

It is assumed that the value of α_a is chosen to maximize expression (2.5), the expected value of the objective function assuming optimal <u>ex post</u> behavior.

The effect of increased uncertainty in the distribution of the random variable θ on (1) the expected value of the objective function and (2) optimal values of the <u>ex ante</u> control variables is derived.

Following the terminology in Diamond and Stiglitz [1974] a family of distribution functions $F(\theta,r)$ differentiable in r such that

$$f(\theta,r) \equiv F_\theta(\theta,r)$$

and

$$F_\theta(\theta,r) = 0 \quad \text{for} \quad \theta \notin [a,b]$$

is considered. Two distributions $F(\theta,\ r_1)$ and $F(\theta,\ r_2)$ where $r_2 \geq r_1$ satisfy the two conditions

$$(2.6) \qquad \int_a^b [F(\theta,\ r_2) - F(\theta,\ r_1)]d\theta = 0$$

and

$$(2.7) \qquad \int_a^y [F(\theta,\ r_2) - F(\theta,\ r_1)]d\theta \geq 0\ , \quad \forall y \in [a,b]\ .$$

Following Rothschild and Stiglitz [1970] the distribution $F(\theta,\ r_2)$ is spoken of as "riskier" or "more uncertain" than $F(\theta,\ r_1)$; i.e., an increase in r represents an increase in the "riskiness" of θ .

By taking the limit as $r_2 - r_1 \to 0$ expressions (2.6) and (2.7) imply:

$$(2.6') \qquad \int_a^b F_r(\theta,r)d\theta = 0$$

and

$$(2.7') \qquad \int_a^y F_r(\theta,r)d\theta \geq 0 \, , \quad y \in [a,b] \, .$$

Again following Diamond and Stiglitz [1974] define

$$T(y,r) \equiv \int_a^y F_r(\theta,r)d\theta \geq 0 \, , \quad y \in [a,b] \, .$$

Theorem 1. The effect of increased uncertainty in the distribution of θ is given by the sign of $W_{\theta\theta}$.

Proof. Consider a given vector $\bar{\alpha}_a$. The effect of increased uncertainty on

$$\int_a^b W(\bar{\alpha}_a, \theta)F_\theta(\theta,r)d\theta$$

is

$$(2.8) \qquad \frac{d\int_a^b W(\bar{\alpha}_a, \theta)F_\theta(\theta,r)d\theta}{dr} \, .$$

Differentiation and integration by parts yields

$$(2.9)\qquad \int_a^b W(\overline{\alpha}_a,\ \theta)F_{\theta r}(\theta,r)d\theta$$

$$= -\int W_\theta(\overline{\alpha}_a,\ \theta)F_r(\theta,r)d\theta$$

$$= \int W_{\theta\theta}(\overline{\alpha}_a,\ \theta)T(\theta,r)d\theta$$

since $F_r(a,r) = F_r(b,r) = T(a,r) = T(b,r) = 0$. Since $T(\theta,r) \geq 0$ for all θ expression (2.9) has the same sign as $W_{\theta\theta}(\overline{\alpha}_a,\ \theta)$ if $W_{\theta\theta}(\theta,r)$ is uniformly signed for $\theta \in [a,b]$.

Increased uncertainty will, in general, affect the optimal value of α_a . Let α_{a1} represent the optimal value of α_a for $r = r_1$ and α_{a2} the optimal value of α_a for $r = r_2$, $r_2 > r_1$. Then if $W_{\theta\theta} \geq 0$

$$\int W(\alpha_{a2},\ \theta)F_\theta(\theta,\ r_2)d\theta$$

$$\geq \int W(\alpha_{a1},\ \theta)F_\theta(\theta,\ r_2)d\theta$$

$$\geq \int W(\alpha_{a1},\ \theta)F_\theta(\theta,\ r_1)d\theta\ .$$

Similarly if $W_{\theta\theta} \leq 0$

$$\int W(\alpha_{a1},\ \theta)F_\theta(\theta,\ r_1)d\theta$$

$$\geq \int W(\alpha_{a2},\ \theta)F_\theta(\theta,\ r_1)d\theta$$

$$\geq \int W(\alpha_{a2},\ \theta)F_\theta(\theta,\ r_2)d\theta\ . \qquad \square$$

Adjusting the values of the _ex ante_ controls may affect the _magnitude_ but not change the direction of the effect of increased uncertainty.

To determine the effect of increased uncertainty in θ on the expected value of the objective function differentiate both sides of expression (2.4) twice with respect to θ to obtain:

$$(2.10)\qquad W_{\theta\theta} = \sum_{i=k+1}^{n} V_{\alpha_i} \frac{d^2\alpha_i}{d\theta^2} + \sum_{i,j=k+1}^{n} V_{\alpha_i\alpha_j}\left(\frac{d\alpha_i}{d\theta}\right)\left(\frac{d\alpha_j}{d\theta}\right)$$

$$+ 2\sum_{i=k+1}^{n} V_{\alpha_i\theta}\left(\frac{d\alpha_i}{d\theta}\right) + V_{\theta\theta} .$$

The first-order conditions (2.2) imply that the first term is 0 . Differentiating (2.2) with respect to θ yields

$$(2.11)\qquad \sum_{j=k+1}^{n} V_{\alpha_i\alpha_j}\frac{d\alpha_j}{d\theta} + V_{\alpha_i\theta} = 0$$

implying

$$(2.12)\qquad \frac{d\alpha_p}{d\theta} = -\{V_{\alpha_i\,\alpha_j}\}^{-1} V_{\alpha_p\theta}$$

where

$$V_{\alpha_p\theta} \equiv \begin{bmatrix} V_{\alpha_j\theta} \end{bmatrix}, \qquad j = k+1, \ldots, n .$$

Without loss of generality one may restrict the analysis to a set of n-k "orthogonal" <u>ex post</u> controls for which:

$$V_{\alpha_i\alpha_j} = 0 , \quad i \neq j .$$

In this case expression (2.12) reduces to

$$(2.12')\qquad \frac{d\alpha_i}{d\theta} = -\frac{V_{\alpha_i\theta}}{V_{\alpha_i\alpha_i}} , \quad i = k+1, \ldots, n$$

and expression (2.10) becomes

$$(2.10') \qquad - \sum_{i=k+1}^{n} \frac{(V_{\alpha_i \theta})^2}{V_{\alpha_i \alpha_i}} + V_{\theta\theta} \ .$$

The first term is necessarily nonnegative while the second term is negative if the objective function is concave in θ . Note, however, that the concavity of V in θ is not sufficient for the negativity of (2.10') if $k < n$, that is, if there is a positive number of _ex post_ controls.

The term $(V_{\alpha_i \theta})^2$ indicates the degree to which the control variable α_i can offset the effect of the random variable θ on the objective. The term $V_{\alpha_i \alpha_i}$ reflects the cost of moving the control variable α_i while $V_{\theta\theta}$ represents the direct effect, holding the values of all controls constant, of increased variation in θ on the objective.

On the basis of (2.10') one may observe that the effect of increased uncertainty on the expected value of the objective function is more likely to be positive (1) the larger the number of _ex post_ controls, (2) the greater the interaction between the _ex post_ controls and the random term in affecting the objective, (3) the lower the cost of adjusting the _ex post_ controls, and (4) the lower the direct effect of variations in θ on V .

Consider that the control variable α_i must be set at time t_i where $t_i \leq t_j$ for $i < j$ and that the true value of θ becomes known at time t_θ . The control variables for which $t_i \geq t_\theta$ may naturally be considered _ex post_ controls while those for which $t_i < t_\theta$ may be thought of as _ex ante_ controls.

This structure provides a natural definition for the value of information available at time t .

Definition 2.1. The ex ante value of the datum μ available at time t_μ , $Z(\mu, t_\mu)$ is given by the expression

$$(2.13) \qquad Z(\mu, t_\mu) = \max_{\alpha_i : t_i < t_\mu} \int_a^b \{\int \max_{\alpha_j : t_\mu \le t_j < t_\theta} \int_a^b W(\alpha_a, \theta) f(\theta/\mu) d\theta] g(\mu) d\mu\} f(x) dx - \max_{\alpha_i : t_i < t_\theta} \int_a^b W(\alpha_a, \theta) f(\theta) d\theta$$

where $g(\mu)$ represents the prior probability density function of the datum μ .

Observe that the datum (μ, t_μ) is worthless (1) if $f(\theta/\mu) = f(\theta)$, in which case it is irrelevant or (2) if $\{\alpha_j : t_\mu < t_j < t_\theta\} = \emptyset$, in which case it is untimely. Information which does not affect value of control variables is of no value. The reduction of uncertainty or increase in knowledge for its own sake is not valued under the present assumptions.

A special case of definition 2.1 presented by Gould [1974]: only a single control variable is considered and the datum is the actual value θ^* of the random variable θ . In this case expression (2.13) reduces to

$$(2.13') \qquad \int_a^b \max_\alpha W(\alpha, \theta) f(\theta) d\theta - \max_\alpha \int_a^b W(\alpha, \theta) f(\theta) d\theta$$

assuming $t_\mu \le t < t_\theta$.

Gould demonstrates that, in general, the effect of increased uncertainty in the random variable θ on expression (2.13') is ambiguous but if W is a linear function of θ increased uncertainty increases the value of information. We derive a slightly weaker condition for increased uncertainty to increase the value of information:

<u>Theorem 2</u>. Increased uncertainty in the distribution of θ increases the value of information when the derivative of the objective function with respect to the control variable α is linear in the random variable θ .

<u>Proof</u>. Consider, as before, a family of probability distributions $F(\theta,r)$ increasing in θ on $\theta \in [a,b]$ with $F_\theta = 0$ elsewhere and satisfying conditions (2.6') and (2.7') above. The effect of increased uncertainty is given by

$$(2.14) \qquad \frac{d\int_a^b [W(\alpha(\theta), \theta) - W(\alpha^*, \theta)]F_\theta(\theta,r)d\theta}{dr}$$

where $\alpha(\theta)$ is implicitly defined by:

$$(2.15) \qquad W_\alpha(\alpha, \theta) = 0$$

and α^* is the solution to

$$(2.16) \qquad \int_a^b W_\alpha(\alpha, \theta)F_\theta(\theta,r)d\theta = 0 \ .$$

Differentiation yields

$$(2.17) \quad \int_a^b \left[- \frac{W_{\alpha\theta}^2}{W_{\alpha\alpha}} + W_{\theta\theta}(\alpha(\theta), \theta) - W_{\theta\theta}(\alpha^*, \theta) \right] T(\theta,r)d\theta - \int_a^b W_\alpha(\alpha^*, \theta)\frac{d\alpha^*}{dr}F_\theta d\theta \ .$$

Differentiating condition (2.16)

$$(2.18) \qquad \frac{d\alpha^*}{dr} = \frac{-\int_a^b W_{\alpha\theta\theta} T(\theta,r)d\theta}{\int_a^b W_{\alpha\alpha} F_\theta d\theta}$$

which is independent of θ. Thus, from condition (2.16) the second integral in expression (2.17) is zero. The effect of increased uncertainty is given by the sign of

$$(2.19) \qquad \frac{-(W_{\alpha\theta})^2}{W_{\alpha\alpha}} + W_{\theta\theta}(\alpha(\theta),\ \theta) - W_{\theta\theta}(\alpha^*,\ \theta)\ .$$

The first term is always positive. If $W_{\alpha\theta\theta} = 0$ the second and third terms cancel. □

We now consider the effect of increased uncertainty on the optimal value of ex ante controls. In the case of a single control variable α Rothschild and Stiglitz [1971] demonstrated the following result:

Theorem 3. (Rothschild-Stiglitz) The effect of increased uncertainty in the distribution of a random variable θ on the optimal value of the single ex ante control α is given by the sign of $W_{\alpha\theta\theta}$ when it is of uniform sign.

Proof. Differentiating the first-order condition for a maximum,

$$\int_a^b W_\alpha(\alpha,\theta)F_\theta(\theta,r)d\theta = 0\ ,$$

with respect to r yields

$$\frac{d\alpha^*}{dr} = \frac{-\int_a^b W_{\alpha\theta\theta} T(\theta,r)\,d\theta}{\int_a^b W_{\alpha\alpha} F_\theta(\theta,r)\,d\theta} .$$

The denominator, from the second-order condition for a maximum, is negative. Thus, since $T(\theta,r) \geq 0$, the sign of $d\alpha^*/dr$ is the same as that of $W_{\alpha\theta\theta}$ if it is of uniform sign. □

We now consider the case in which the number of ex ante controls exceeds one.

Theorem 4. The effect of increased uncertainty in the distribution of a random variable θ on the optimal value of an ex ante control α_i is given by the sign of the ith component of the vector

$$(2.20) \qquad \frac{d\alpha^*}{dr} = \{\bar{W}_{\alpha_i\alpha_j}\}^{-1}[-W_{\alpha_a\theta\theta}]$$

where

$$\bar{W}_{ij} \equiv \int_a^b W_{\alpha_i\alpha_j} F_\theta\, d\theta .$$

Proof. Differentiating the k equations of the first-order conditions for a maximum yields

$$(2.21) \quad \sum_{j=1}^{k} \int_a^b W_{\alpha_i\alpha_j}(\theta,r)\left(\frac{d\alpha_i^*}{dr}\right) F_\theta\, d\theta + \int_a^b W_{\alpha_i\theta\theta} T(\theta,r)\,d\theta = 0 \quad \text{if} \quad i = 1, \ldots, k .$$

Solving for $d\alpha_j^*/dr$ gives

$$\frac{d\alpha^*}{dr} = \{\overline{W}_{ij}\}^{-1}\left[-\int_a^b W_{\alpha_a\theta\theta}T(\theta,r)d\theta\right] .$$

If $W_{\alpha_i\theta\theta}$ is uniformly signed for each $i = 1, \ldots, k$ then $d\alpha_a^*/dr$ has the same sign as

$$-(|\{\overline{W}_{ij}\}|)^{-1}\left[\sum_{j=1}^{k} \Delta_{ij}W_{\alpha_j\theta\theta}\right]$$

where Δ_{ij} represents the cofactor of $\overline{W}_{ij}$ in the Hessian matrix. □

For the case in which the ex ante controls are orthogonal, i.e., if $\overline{W}_{ij} = 0$ for $i \neq j$, condition (2.19) reduces to the condition in Theorem 1.

For the case $k = 2$ the effect of increased uncertainty on the control variable α_1 is given by the sign of

(2.22) $$-\overline{W}_{22}W_{\alpha_1\theta\theta} + \overline{W}_{12}W_{\alpha_2\theta\theta} .$$

III. Uncertain Production and Stabilization

This section illustrates some of the results in the previous section in a general equilibrium two-sector model with a multiplicative uncertain term in the production relationship. Social welfare is a function $U(x_1, x_2)$ of the output of two commodities x_1 and x_2. Production is described by the relationship

$$x_2 = \theta f(x_1) \tag{3.1}$$

where $f > 0$, $f' < 0$ and $f'' \leq 0$ and θ is a random variable with distribution $F(\theta)$ for which $F(0) = 0$, $F(b) = 1$ for some $0 < b < \infty$. We assume $E(\theta) \equiv \bar{\theta} = 1$.

The objective function may be written as

$$E\{U[x_1, \theta f(x_1)]\} . \tag{3.2}$$

The single control variable is x_1. First the effect of increased uncertainty on welfare and on production (1) when x_1 is an *ex ante* control and (2) when x_1 is an *ex post* control is considered. Then the welfare effects of price stabilization under each regime and the value of technological information are derived.

A. <u>Production as an ex ante Control</u>

Production of commodity 1 is chosen to maximize

(3.3) $$E\{U[x_1, \theta f(x_1)]\} \equiv E[W(x_1, \theta)] .$$

Differentiating W twice with respect to θ yields

$$W_{\theta\theta} = U_{22}f(x_1)^2$$

which, if marginal utility is diminishing, is negative. Hence:

<u>Proposition 1</u>. Increased production uncertainty reduces expected utility when production is an <u>ex ante</u> control.

The effect of increased uncertainty on the optimal value of x_1 is given by the sign of

(3.4) $$W_{x_1\theta\theta} = f(x_1)[2U_{22}f'(x_1) + U_{222}f'(x_1)f(x_1) + U_{221}f(x_1)]$$

which is generally ambiguous. For the class of utility functions

(3.5) $$U(x_1, x_2) = (1/\gamma)[x_1^\gamma + x_2^\gamma] , \quad \gamma < 1$$

expression (3.4) is negative for $0 < \gamma < 1$ and positive for $\gamma < 0$; when marginal utility diminishes at a rapid rate, increased uncertainty is more likely to increase production of the commodity with uncertain technology.

B. Production as an *ex post* Control

When x_1 may be chosen once θ is known the effect of increased uncertainty on expected welfare is given by the sign of

$$(3.6) \qquad U_{22}(f)^2 - \frac{[U_{12}f + U_{22}\theta f'f + U_2 f']^2}{[U_{11} + 2U_{12}\theta f' + U_{22}(\theta f')^2 + U_2\theta f'']}$$

which has a negative first term and positive second term. If the utility function is additively separable and if the production technology is linear with $f' = 1$ expression (3.6) has the same sign as

$$(3.7) \qquad (U_2)^2\left[\frac{2U_{22}\theta f}{U_2} + 1\right] - U_{11}U_{22} \ .$$

The second-order condition for a maximum implies the second term is negative. The first term is positive if the elasticity of marginal utility of commodity 2 is less than one-half. One may conclude

Proposition 2. If production is an *ex post* control a necessary condition for an increase in uncertainty to increase expected utility function is that the elasticity of the marginal utility of commodity 2 not exceed one-half. If this necessary condition is met increased uncertainty is more likely to increase utility the greater the marginal utility of commodity 2.

Proposition 2 implies that, when the allocation of resources may occur with knowledge of actual productivity in the sector producing commodity 2 increased variability in production may be desirable even if utility functions are concave.

C. The Welfare Effects of Price Stabilization

Suppose that commodities 1 and 2 may be stored costlessly and that utility is intertemporally, additively separable. In this section it is shown that a commodity price stabilization scheme will necessarily increase expected welfare when production is an *ex ante* control but the effect on expected welfare is ambiguous when the production decision occurs *ex post*.

First consider the case of production as an ***ex ante*** control. Assume that a price stabilization program attempts to fix a price $\bar{p}$ of commodity 2 relative to commodity 1 and that consumption of commodity 2 cannot exceed expected production. Let x_1^* represent commodity 1 production and, hence, $f(x_1^*)$ expected commodity 2 production. Unless production and consumption are completely specialized in one commodity utility maximization by consumers implies

$$(3.8) \qquad \bar{p} = \frac{U_2(x_1^*, f(x_1^*))}{U_1(x_1^*, f(x_1^*))}$$

while profit maximization by producers implies:

$$(3.9) \qquad E[1 + \bar{p}\theta f'(x_1^*)] = 1 + \bar{p}f' = 0 .$$

Conditions (3.8) and (3.9) together imply the first-order condition for a social optimum when the production relationship is certain, i.e.,

$$(3.10) \qquad U_1 + f'(x_1^*)U_2 = 0 .$$

Since increased uncertainty reduces expected welfare the price stabilization project, by creating a situation identical to that of complete certainty in production, increases expected social welfare.

When production is an *ex post* control, however, the welfare effect of a price stabilization program is ambiguous. Assume that the utility function is of the form

$$(3.11) \qquad U(x_1, x_2) = \frac{1}{\gamma}(x_1^{\gamma} + x_2^{\gamma}) ,$$

that the transformation surface is given by

$$(3.12) \qquad x_2 = \theta(\bar{x} - x_1) , \quad x_1, x_2 \geq 0 ,$$

and that $g(\theta)$ is uniformly distributed on $[0,2]$.

When a price p is established by a price stabilization program profit maximization implies:

$$(3.13) \qquad x_1 = \bar{x} , \quad x_2 = 0 \quad \text{if} \quad \theta > p$$

and

$$x_1 = 0 , \quad x_2 = \theta\bar{x} \quad \text{if} \quad \theta < p .$$[1]

These conditions in turn imply that

$$(3.14) \qquad E(x_1) \equiv \bar{x}_1 = [1 - F(p)]\bar{x} = (2 - p)\bar{x}/2 \; ; \quad 0 \leq p \leq 2$$
$$= 0 \; ; \quad p < 0$$
$$= \bar{x} \; ; \quad p > 2$$

[1]Note that price stabilization destabilizes production when production is an *ex post* control. Without price stabilization production is always incompletely specialized as long as $\theta U_2/U_1 = 1$ for $x_1 > 0$, $x_2 > 0$. With the stabilization scheme production is almost always completely specialized.

and

$$(3.15)\qquad E(x_2) = \bar{x}_2 = \bar{x}\int_0^p \theta F_\theta d\theta = p\bar{x}/2 \;;\quad 0 < p < 2$$
$$= \bar{x} \;;\quad p > 2$$
$$= 0 \;;\quad p < 0 .$$

Utility maximization implies

$$(3.16)\qquad p = \frac{U_2(\bar{x}_1, \bar{x}_2)}{U_1(\bar{x}_1, \bar{x}_2)} = \left[\frac{p}{(2 - p)}\right]^{\gamma-1}$$

which has as a solution $p = 1$. This solution is unique since

$$\frac{d\left[\left(\frac{2 - p}{p}\right)^{1-\gamma} - p\right]}{dp}$$

is negative everywhere on $p \in [0,2]$, and the optimum p cannot lie outside $p \in [0,2]$ if positive consumption of both commodities is desired.

When the price is set at $p = 1$ expected utility is given by

$$(3.17)\qquad U = \left(\frac{\bar{x}^{\gamma}}{\gamma}\right)2^{1-\gamma} .$$

Without the price stabilization program a competitive equilibrium is characterized by

$$(3.18)\qquad U_1 + \theta f'(x_1)U_2 = 0 .$$

Assuming preferences and technology represented by (3.11) and (3.12) respectively, this condition implies

$$x_1 = \bar{x}(\theta^{\gamma/1-\gamma} + 1)^{-1} \tag{3.19}$$

$$x_2 = \theta^{1/1-\gamma}\bar{x}(\theta^{\gamma/1-\gamma} + 1)^{-1} .$$

The unstabilized price is given by

$$p(\theta) = \frac{U_2}{U_1} = \theta \tag{3.20}$$

and utility by

$$U(\theta) = \left(\frac{\bar{x}^{\gamma}}{\gamma}\right)(\theta^{\gamma/1-\gamma} + 1)^{1-\gamma} . \tag{3.21}$$

The price stabilization program will increase or decrease expected utility as

$$U - E[U(\theta)] \gtrless 0 \tag{3.22}$$

or, as

$$2^{1-\gamma} \gtrless E[(\theta^{\gamma/1-\gamma} + 1)^{1-\gamma}] \equiv E[h(\theta)] . \tag{3.23}$$

If $\theta = \bar{\theta} = 1$ with probability 1, expression (3.23) is an equality. The effect on expected welfare of the price stabilization scheme by Jensen's inequality hence depends on the convexity or concavity of $h(\theta)$. Differentiating twice yields an expression with the same sign as

$$[(\gamma-1)\theta^{\gamma/1-\gamma} + (2\gamma - 1)/1-\gamma] . \tag{3.24}$$

The first term is negative while the second is positive if $\gamma > 1/2$. For low levels of uncertainty θ is very near 1. Expression (3.24) then has the same sign as

$$(3.25) \qquad -\gamma^2 + 4\gamma - 2$$

which is positive when $\gamma > 2 - \sqrt{2} = .586$. One may conclude that the price stabilization scheme will increase expected welfare even when production is an <u>ex post</u> control unless the degree of relative risk aversion is somewhat above one half.

From expression (3.20) observe that, when production is an <u>ex post</u> control, the expected price without the price stabilization scheme is the same as the stabilized price:without stabilization the price is simply the realized marginal rate of transformation which has an expected value of unity. From the solution to condition (3.16) the only sustainable stabilized price is also unity.[2]

When production is an <u>ex ante</u> control, however, the expected price without stabilization is greater than the sustainable stabilized price. With stabilization the condition for expected profit maximization, expression (3.9), implies $\bar{p} = 1$ if there is to be incomplete specialization.

Without stabilization

$$(3.26) \qquad p = \left[\frac{\theta(\bar{x} - x_1^*)}{x_1^*}\right]^{\gamma-1} .$$

From the first-order condition for a maximum

$$(3.27) \qquad x_1^* = \bar{x}(1+y^{1/1-\gamma})^{-1}$$

where

---

[2]The equality of the expected price without stabilization and the unique sustainable stabilized price does not generalize to situations with non-linear technologies.

$$y = E(\theta^{\gamma}) .$$

Substituting (3.27) into (3.26)

$$p(\theta) = \theta^{\gamma-1}[E(\theta^{\gamma})]^{-1} \tag{3.28}$$

so that

$$E(p) = E(\theta^{\gamma-1})/E(\theta^{\gamma}) \tag{3.29}$$

which is greater than 1 since

$$E(\theta^{\gamma-1}) \geq 1$$

and

$$0 < E(\theta^{\gamma}) < 1 .$$

Under the present assumptions the price stabilization program reduces the expected price of commodity 2 when production is an <u>ex ante</u> control.

D. The Value of Information on Technology

The value of knowledge of the true value of θ prior to deciding x_1 is

$$(3.30) \qquad \int_0^b U[x_1(\theta),\ \theta f(x_1(\theta))]F_\theta d\theta - \max_{x_1} \int_0^b U[x_1,\ \theta f(x_1)]F_\theta d\theta$$

where $x(\theta)$ is defined by

$$U_1 + U_2 \theta f'(x_1) = 0 .$$

Under assumptions (3.11) about preferences and (3.12) about technology expression (3.30) becomes

$$(3.31) \qquad \frac{\bar{x}^\gamma}{\gamma}\{E[(1+\theta^{\gamma/1-\gamma})^{1-\gamma}] - [1+E(\theta^\gamma)^{1/1-\gamma}]^{1-\gamma}\}$$

which is positive for all values of γ except $\gamma = 0$. When $\gamma = 0$, $x_1^* = \bar{x}/2$ independent of the marginal rate of transformation.

IV. Summary

The theme of this essay, as developed in a general optimizing model and in a model with stochastic production, is that increases in the variation of exogenous parameters need not reduce expected welfare when actions may be taken in response to actual outcomes. Viewed in this light, perhaps what is termed "uncertainty" would better be called "variability." Increased variability results in increased uncertainty only when actions must precede knowledge of outcomes. Aversion to risk implies that, to the extent one must act without knowledge, one would prefer certainty to uncertainty in a parameter which enters a concave objective function. One would prefer to live in a world characterized by variation rather than uniformity, nevertheless. This essay has suggested how variability, by itself, can increase rather than diminish expected welfare. When economic systems are flexible in their responses to changing circumstances, the variability of the world, seen as the curse of uncertainty when no *ex post* controls are available, is transformed into an aspect of nature's bounty.

BIBLIOGRAPHY

Arrow, K. J. [1971]. "The Value of and Demand for Information," Essays in the Theory of Risk Bearing (Chicago: Markham).

Diamond, P. A. and J. E. Stiglitz [1974]. "Increases in Risk and in Risk Aversion," Journal of Economic Theory, 8, pp. 337-360.

Gould, J. P. [1974]. "Risk, Stochastic Preference, and the Value of Information," Journal of Economic Theory, 8, pp. 64-84.

Hadar, J. and W. Russell [1969]. "Rules for Ordering Uncertain Prospects," American Economic Review, 59, pp. 25-34.

Oi, W. Y. [1961]. "The Desirability of Price Instability under Perfect Competition," Econometrica, 30, pp. 729-743.

Rothschild, M. and J. E. Stiglitz [1970]. "Increasing Risk I. A Definition," Journal of Economic Theory, 2, pp. 225-243.

__________ [1971]. "Increasing Risk: II. Its Economic Consequences," Journal of Economic Theory, 3, pp. 66-84.

Samuelson, P. A. [1972]. "Feasible Price Stability," Quarterly Journal of Economics, 86, pp. 476-493.

Waugh, F. V. [1944]. "Does the Consumer Benefit From Price Instability," Quarterly Journal of Economics, 58, pp. 602-614.

ESSAY II

SAVINGS AND RELATIVE PRICE UNCERTAINTY

I. Introduction: Uncertainty, Welfare and Savings

Uncertainty about future states of nature was formally introduced into general equilibrium theory in the form of contingent-commodity markets. According to Debreu [1959, Chapter 7], if the consumer is able to purchase any commodity for delivery only in the event of a particular state of nature, uncertainty may be treated in the same general equilibrium model applied to the deterministic world. The only requirement is that a market exist for each physical commodity for each state of nature. Under this regime the household may be certain of its level of consumption of any commodity, at any moment, in any state of nature. If m_i is the number of states of nature at time i, if n_i is the number of physical commodities at time i, and if T is the number of time periods $\sum_{i=1}^{T} n_i \times m_i$ markets are required. Arrow [1963] has shown that, under certain restrictions on preferences, the existence of a set of securities spanning all states of nature will yield an outcome equivalent to Debreu's. The number of markets or securities required is reduced to $\sum_{i=1}^{T} m_i$.

Radner [1968] has emphasized that, because of the transactions costs involved in establishing contingent commodity markets and because not all economic agents have equal access to information on the actual state of nature (the familiar problem of "moral hazard") a complete set of contingent-commodity markets or of Arrow securities is unlikely to appear. He argues that this failure will result in the opening of spot markets at future dates as information on states of nature becomes available. The existence of such spot markets creates both (a) a demand for assets (savings) which may be traded for commodities in these markets and (b) uncertainty about the prices at which commodities are traded in these markets. It is in such a regime, in which the household (a) cannot sell uncertain future endowments in forward contingent-commodities markets, (b) is uncertain of the future value of his assets in terms of consumption goods, (c) is uncertain of relative future prices, and (d) does not know his own needs in future periods, that savings behavior under uncertainty becomes of interest.

The effect on savings of increased uncertainty of the first type, that due to uncertainty of the value of future endowments, has been considered by Leland [1968] in a two-period model and by Sibley [1975] in a multi-period context. Uncertainty about the value of savings relative to the price of all consumption goods in future periods has been analyzed by Levhari and Srinivasan [1969], Hahn [1970], Sandmo [1970], Mirman [1971], Mirrlees [1971], Rothschild and Stiglitz [1971], and Merton [1969 and 1971]. These studies all assume that the utility function is intertemporally-additively separable. Kihlstrom and Mirman [1974] have considered optimal savings and consumption when interest rates are uncertain under alternative assumptions about the substitutability of consumption among periods.

Stiglitz [1972] and Fischer [1975] have analyzed optimal portfolio choice when future relative prices are uncertain but when there exists for each uncertain price an asset with rate of return perfectly correlated with it while Epstein [1975] presents a theoretical framework for treating the savings-consumption decision under uncertainty in a multiproduct context when only a single asset is available. None of these studies considers the effect of uncertainty in the future <u>relative</u> price of a particular physical commodity on optimal savings. The purpose of this essay is to explore this problem in several contexts.

Section II develops a general framework for analyzing expected-utility maximization in a two-period multi-commodity and multi-asset environment in which prices and income in the second period are stochastic. This framework is then applied to consider the effect of changes in the subjective probability distribution of the price of a particular commodity on optimal savings and expected welfare when the selection of assets available to consumers does not span the space of price variation.

Leland [1968] and Sandmo [1970] find that increased uncertainty in future non-wealth income will generate increased savings among consumers whose utility functions are characterized by decreasing absolute risk aversion. Hahn [1970] and Rothschild and Stiglitz [1971] show that, for the class of utility functions characterized by constant relative risk aversion, increased uncertainty in the rate of return on wealth increases savings for those with degree of relative risk aversion greater than unity and lowers it for those less risk averse. The present study finds that, for the case of constant relative risk aversion, increased uncertainty in the relative price of a commodity increases optimal savings when the degree of relative risk aversion is either less than unity or very large. For relative risk aversion in a neighborhood bounded below by unity and above at some finite level increases in relative price uncertainty may lower optimal savings. Another factor besides the degree of risk aversion influencing the direction of the relationship between relative price uncertainty and savings is the substitutability between the commodity whose price becomes more uncertain and alternative commodities. When the price and income elasticities of demand for the commodity in question are high a negative relationship between price uncertainty and savings is more likely to arise.

Section III of this essay treats the relationship between savings and relative price uncertainty when assets with rates of return perfectly correlated with each commodity's price are available. In the two-period context it is found that, in the case of constant relative risk aversion, savings is greater than in the one-asset case for consumers with degree of relative risk aversion less than unity and lower for those more risk averse.

Both Sections II and III deal primarily with the case in which utility is intertemporally-additively separable. The implications of several alternative specifications are also explored.

Section IV considers the effect of increased relative price uncertainty in a multiperiod context. On the one hand if increased uncertainty is anticipated in only one period the considerations affecting the optimal response of savings differ in general from those in the two-period case. On the other hand if the increased uncertainty is expected to apply to all remaining periods in one's lifetime the effect on optimal consumption of increased uncertainty on consumption behavior, for the case of Cobb-Douglas iso-elastic marginal utility at least, is the same as under the two-period assumption.

The relationship between price uncertainty and expected consumer welfare has been discussed by Waugh [1944] and Samuelson [1972]. The first author demonstrates that if the marginal utility of income or the marginal utility of other consumption is constant increased uncertainty in the relative price of a commodity will increase the expected utility of a consumer.

Section II demonstrates that increased relative price uncertainty will increase expected utility when the price and income elasticities of demand for the commodity are large relative to the degree of relative risk aversion and the share in total consumption of the commodity in question. Otherwise the income effect of increased price uncertainty will lower expected utility. In Section III it is shown that if an asset is available for each commodity then increased price uncertainty will always increase the expected utility of the consumer. This is also the case in the multiperiod context discussed in Section IV if the marginal utility of income is constant in some subsequent period in which the price distribution is unchanged.

II. Relative Price Uncertainty and Savings with One Asset: Two-Period Analysis

Assume the existence of n physical commodities which may be consumed either in one or both of two periods. Consumption of commodity j in period i is denoted c_j^i and the level of utility is given by

$$(2.1) \qquad U(\ldots c_j^i \ldots) , \quad i = 1, 2 ; \quad j = 1, \ldots, n .$$

The function u is quasi-concave and increasing in each argument. Exogenous income in period i is denoted y^i .

Assume commodities may only be consumed in nonnegative amounts and in the period in which they are purchased. Transfer of expenditure between periods may occur through the purchase, in possibly negative quantities, of assets a_i , in period 1 for sale in period 2 .

Prices of all commodities and assets in period 1 are set at unity. The price of commodity j in period 2 is p_j and of asset i in period 2 is r_i . Purchases and sales must satisfy the two budget constraints

$$(2.2a) \qquad \sum_{j=1}^{n} c_j^1 + \sum_{i=1}^{m} a_i - y^1 = 0$$

$$(2.2b) \qquad \sum_{j=1}^{n} p_j c_j^2 - \sum_{i=1}^{m} r_i a_i - y^2 = 0 .$$

Assets and commodities for period 1 consumption are purchased with knowledge of actual period 1 prices and income but without complete information about prices and income in period 2. Commodity purchases in period 2, however, are made with this information. In terms of the terminology of the first essay, c_j^1 and a_i are <u>ex ante</u> controls with respect to the random variables y^2 , p_j and r_i while c_j^2 are *ex post* controls.

For given values of the *ex ante* controls and the realized values of the random variables the optimizing household selects c_j^2 to maximize the utility function (2.1) subject to the period 2 budget constraint (2.2b). The *ex post* utility function is thus defined as:

$$(2.3) \qquad V(c^1, a, r, y^2, p) = \max_{c_2} U(c_1, c_2)$$

subject to

$$(2.2b) \qquad p'c^2 - r'a - y^2 = 0 \ .$$

Epstein's [1975] variable indirect utility function is the same as our *ex post* utility function for the case in which the number of assets is one.

Assets contribute to welfare only through their contribution to expenditure in period 2. Thus expression (2.3) may be rewritten as

$$(2.3') \qquad V(c^1, r'a + y^2, p) \ .$$

The household is assumed to choose values of the *ex ante* controls, c^1 and a , to maximize the expected value of (2.3') subject to the budget constraint in period 1, expression (2.2a).

This essay considers the effect of changes in the distribution of a price of a particular commodity, commodity 2, on welfare and on optimal savings. Other commodities have a known period 2 price of unity and are aggregated into a Hicks composite commodity, commodity 1. Initially, it is assumed that only a single asset, "money," held in amount s and with a price in period 2 of unity, is available. Period 2 income, y^2, is also known with certainty in terms of the price of commodity 1 or savings. Risky income and interest rate are considered in Part C while Section III introduces alternative, risky assets.

The price in period 2 of commodity 2, in terms of commodity 1 or money, is a random variable p which has probability distribution $F(p)$ with the following properties:

$$
\begin{aligned}
(2.4) \qquad & F(0) = 0 \\
& F(\hat{p}) = 1 \quad \text{for some} \quad 0 < \hat{p} < \infty \\
& f(p) \equiv F'(p) \geq 0 \\
& \bar{p} \equiv E(p) = \int_0^{\hat{p}} pf(p)dp = 1 \, .
\end{aligned}
$$

The effects of three types of modifications in the distribution function $F(p)$ on optimal savings and welfare are considered. First treated is the effect of changing the distribution from $F(p)$ to $G(p)$ where $G(p) \leq F(p)$ for all p and where $G(p) < F(p)$ for at least one p. This relationship between G and F is that of first-order stochastic dominance discussed by Hadar and Russell [1969] and Bawa [1975]. The effect of a mean-preserving spread in the distribution of p discussed by Rothschild and Stiglitz [1970] is analyzed second. Comparing two distributions $F(p, r_1)$ and $F(p, r_2)$ where $r_2 \geq r_1$, $F(p, r_2)$ is at least as risky as $F(p, r_1)$ if

$$(2.5) \qquad \int_0^x [F(p, r_2) - F(p, r_1)]dp \geq 0 \, , \quad 0 \leq x \leq \hat{p}$$

while

$$\int_0^{\hat{p}} [F(p, r_2) - F(p, r_1)]dp = 0 .$$

This relationship between $F(p, r_2)$ and $F(p, r_1)$ is a special case of the second-order stochastic dominance discussed by Hadar and Russell [1969] and Bawa [1975]. Finally the mean-utility preserving increase in risk introduced by Diamond and Stiglitz [1974] is analyzed. A mean-utility preserving increase in risk occurs if

(2.6)
$$\int_0^{x} V_p F_r(p,r)dp \geq 0 , \quad 0 \leq x \leq \hat{p}$$

$$\int_0^{\hat{p}} V_p F_r(p,r)dp = 0$$

where

$$F_r(p,r) = \lim_{\delta \to 0} \frac{[F(p, r+\delta) - F(p,r)]}{\delta} .$$

In Part A it is assumed that the utility function (2.1) is characterized by intertemporal additive separability. Part B explores some consequences of relaxing this assumption.

A. Intertemporally Additively Separable Utility

Assume that the utility function (2.1) may be written as

$$(2.1') \qquad U^1(c^1) + U^2(c^2) \ .$$

The first-order conditions for optimal values of c^2 are independent of the allocation of expenditure on consumption in period 1. The *ex post* utility function may thus be written as

$$(2.7) \qquad U^1(c^1) + V\ (y^2 + s,\ p)$$

where V^2 is simply the indirect utility function in period 2. The first-order conditions for optimal values of c^1 are independent of p. Hence, assuming optimal allocation of consumption expenditure in period 1, one may write (2.7) as

$$(2.8) \qquad V^1(y^1 - s) + V^2(y^2 + s,\ p)$$

where V^1 is the indirect utility function for period 1.

The optimizing household chooses s to maximize the expected value of expression (2.8). The first-order condition for a maximum is given by:

$$(2.9) \qquad V^1_y + E[V^2_y] = 0 \ .$$

Diminishing marginal utility of income in one or both periods, $V^i_{yy} < 0$ for $i = 1$ or $i = 2$ implies that the second-order condition for a maximum

$$(2.10) \qquad V^1_{yy} + E[V^2_{yy}] < 0$$

is satisfied.

The Case of First-Order Stochastic Dominance

The first question considered is "what is the effect on the optimal choice of s of replacing the distribution F(p) by another G(p) where G(p) dominates F(p) in the first-order sense?" or, more informally, "how does an increase in the anticipated price of commodity 2 in period 2 affect optimal savings?"

The effect on optimal savings of replacing the distribution F(p) by G(p) when

$$G(p) \leq F(p)$$

and where the inequality is strict for at least one p is given by the sign of

$$(2.11) \qquad V^2_{yp} \; .$$

The economic significance of this term may be clarified by translating expression (2.11) into an expression involving only derivatives of the indirect utility function with respect to income.

In the n commodity case

$$(2.12) \qquad V_{p_j} = \sum_{i=1}^{n} U_i \left(\frac{\partial x_i}{\partial p_j} \right) , \quad j = 1, \ldots, n$$

which, substituting the Slutsky relation,

$$(2.13) \qquad = \sum_{i=1}^{n} U_i \left[\left(\frac{\partial x_i}{\partial p_j} \right)_{\overline{U}} - x_j \frac{\partial x_i}{\partial y} \right]$$

$$(2.14) \qquad = \sum_{i=1}^{n} U_i \left(\frac{\partial x_i}{\partial p_j} \right)_{\overline{U}} - x_j V_y$$

where $(\partial x_i/\partial p_j)_{\overline{U}}$ represents the compensated price elasticity of demand. The first term in expression (2.14) is necessarily zero since the change in all the x_i caused by the change in p_j is not changing utility. Thus, in the two commodity case, expression (2.12) implies:

$$V_p^2 = -cV_y^2 \tag{2.15}$$

where c denotes commodity 2 consumption in period 2.

Differentiating expression (2.15) once with respect to income gives

$$V_{yp}^2 = -\frac{\partial c}{\partial y} V_y - cV_{yy} \tag{2.16}$$

which, multiplying by (y/cV_y) has the same sign as

$$-\frac{\partial c}{\partial y}\left(\frac{y}{c}\right) - yV_{yy}/V_y = -Z_y + R \tag{2.17}$$

where Z_y is the income elasticity of demand and R the measure of relative risk aversion.[1] We conclude

Proposition 1. The effect of replacing the distribution F(p) of the relative price of commodity 2 by an alternative distribution G(p) where the relationship between G(p) and F(p) is one of first-order stochastic

---

[1]The definition of the degree of relative risk aversion in the multi-commodity case is discussed by Stiglitz [1969] and Kihlstrom and Mirman [1974]. We follow the first author in defining risk aversion in terms of the partial derivatives with respect to income of the indirect utility function. For a given level of money income, y , the degree of risk aversion will in general vary as relative prices vary. In the case of homothetic utility, however, the degrees of relative and absolute risk aversion are independent of relative prices. See the appendix for further discussion.

dominance is to increase (decrease) optimal savings when the degree of relative risk aversion exceeds (is less than) the income elasticity of demand for commodity 2.

Increasing the probability of higher values of p in period 2 reduces the expected real value of income in period 2. This effect tends to increase optimal savings to equate the marginal utility of income in each period. At the same time increased savings increases the demand for commodity 2 in period 2 if the income elasticity of demand is positive. This effect reduces the value of savings in terms of the amount of commodity 1 consumed in period 2. This second effect of increased price corresponds to a "substitution effect" tending to reduce savings while the first effect is an "income effect" tending to increase savings. When utility is a logarithmic function of income $(R = 1)$ savings increases if commodity 2 is a necessity $(Z_y < 1)$ and decreases if it is a luxury $(Z_y > 1)$.

2. <u>The Case of Second-Order Stochastic Dominance: The Mean Preserving Spread</u>

By Theorem 1 of the first essay the effect of a mean-preserving spread on utility is given by the sign of V_{pp}. Differentiating expression (2.15) with respect to p indicates

$$(2.18) \qquad V_{pp} = -\frac{\partial c}{\partial y} V_y - cV_{yp} .$$

Substituting (2.16) for V_{yp}

$$(2.19) \qquad V_{pp} = \left(-\frac{\partial c}{\partial p} + c\frac{\partial c}{\partial y}\right)V_y + c^2 V_{yy} .$$

Multiplying (2.19) by y/c^2V_y, preserving its sign, gives

$$(2.19') \qquad Z_p\left(\frac{y}{c}\right) + Z_y - R$$

where

$$Z_p \equiv -\frac{\partial c}{\partial p}\frac{1}{c},$$

the price elasticity of demand at $p = 1$

$$Z_y \equiv \frac{\partial c}{\partial y}\left(\frac{y}{c}\right)$$

and

$$R \equiv -yV_{yy}/V_y$$

the degree of relative risk aversion. The first two terms, when commodity 2 is not inferior, are positive while the third is negative. The case $R = 0$ is considered by Waugh [1944] and Samuelson [1972]. The assumption of constant marginal utility of income leads to the conclusion that increased price uncertainty increases expected utility. In general one may conclude

Proposition 2. Increased price uncertainty increases (decreases) expected welfare when the product of the price elasticity of demand for commodity 2 and the inverse of the share of commodity 2 in consumption plus the income elasticity of demand for commodity 2 exceeds (is less than) the degree of relative risk aversion.

Unless the demand for commodity 2 is price and income inelastic the consumer may increase his utility by adjusting his consumption of commodity 2 inversely in response to price fluctuations. This effect is greater the greater the substitutability between commodity 1 and commodity 2 or, equivalently, the greater the price and income elasticities of demand.

Now the effect of increased price uncertainty on optimal savings is considered. Applying Theorem 3 of the first essay to obtain the effect of a mean-preserving spread in the distribution of p on savings one differentiates the first-order condition for a maximum, expression (2.9), twice with respect to p, obtaining V_{ypp}. Differentiating equation (2.19) with respect to y yields

$$(2.20) \qquad V_{ypp} = \left[\partial\left(c\frac{\partial c}{\partial y} - \frac{\partial c}{\partial p}\right)\Big/\partial y\right]V_y + \left[3c\frac{\partial c}{\partial y} - \frac{\partial c}{\partial p}\right]V_{yy} + c^2 V_{yyy} .$$

The sign of (2.20) depends on attitudes toward risk and the characteristics of the demand function for commodity 2. Note from the third term, however, that for $V_{yyy} > 0$, a necessary condition for decreasing absolute risk aversion,[2] increased saving due to increased price uncertainty will be more likely the larger c^2.

The second term indicates that, for the risk-averse individual,

---

[2]The Arrow-Pratt measure of absolute risk aversion is $-V_{yy}/V_y$. Decreasing absolute risk aversion implies

$$\partial(-V_{yy}/V_y)/\partial y < 0 .$$

Evaluating this expression yields

$$\frac{-V_{yyy}V_y + (V_{yy})^2}{V_y^2}$$

which is negative only if $V_{yyy} > 0$. This result is derived by Leland [1968].

with $V_{yy} < 0$, increased saving from increased uncertainty is more likely if the income and price elasticities of the commodity are low. If the price elasticity is high substitution possibilities with other commodities are greater. If the income elasticity is high increased saving, by increasing the demand for commodity 2, will increase the exposure of the individual to the effects of price variation. Dividing through condition (2.20) by V_y , thus preserving its sign, shows that for non-inferior commodities an increase in savings resulting from increased price uncertainty is more likely the <u>smaller</u> the Arrow-Pratt measure of absolute risk aversion: $-V_{yy}/V_y$.[3] If $\partial c/\partial y > 0$ an increase in savings increases the demand for commodity 2 in period 2. The more risk-averse individual will reduce savings to reduce demand for commodity 2 in period 2. Conversely, when commodity 2 is Giffen the more risk-averse individual will save more in response to price uncertainty because (1) increased savings reduces his dependence on commodity 2 and (2) close substitutes for commodity 2 are not available. If commodity 2 is inferior but not Giffen the role of risk aversion is ambiguous.

The first term of expression (2.20) indicates that a positive relationship between savings and price uncertainty is more likely if (1) the absolute value of the income elasticity of demand for commodity 2 is high and if (2) the effect on demand of income and price changes increase with income. These effects are independent of the consumer's attitude toward risk. Price uncertainty is more likely to increase the expected value of the marginal utility of income the larger the absolute value of the effect

---

[3] Multiplying (2.20) by y , again preserving the sign, indicates the same relationship with regard to the Arrow-Pratt measure of relative risk aversion $-(y \cdot V_{yy}/V_y)$.

of income on the demand for commodity 2. If the income and price sensitivity of demand increases with income greater savings will increase substitutability among commodities in period 2.

References to some special cases may clarify condition (2.20). Specifically considered are cases in which (a) demand for commodity 2 is price and income inelastic, and the utility function is characterized by (b) constant marginal utility of income, (c) constant relative risk aversion, (d) constant absolute risk aversion, and (e) iso-elastic marginal utility with constant elasticity of substitution among commodities.

a. Price and Income Inelastic Demand

If $\partial c/\partial y = \partial c/\partial p = 0$ expression (2.20) reduces to $c^2 V_{yyy}$ having the same sign as V_{yyy}. Leland [1968] finds that increased income uncertainty increases (decreases) savings if V_{yyy} is positive (negative). Leland's result is thus a special case of (2.20) in which sources of income are supplied inelastically. Since decreasing absolute risk aversion is sufficient for $V_{yyy} > 0$ (see footnote 2 above) (2.20) implies that increased variance in the price of an inelastically demanded or supplied commodity always increases savings.

b. Constant Marginal Utility of Income

Constant marginal utility of income (CMUI) implies $V_{yy} = V_{yyy} = 0$.[4] Furthermore, since from the Slutsky relationship (2.15)

$$-V_p = cV_y$$

---

[4]For the second-order condition for a maximum to be satisfied one must in this case assume diminishing marginal utility of income in period 1.

implying

$$-V_{pyy} = (\partial^2 c/\partial y^2)V_y$$

and since $V_{yy} = 0 = V_{yyp} = V_{pyy}$ CMUI implies $\partial^2 c/\partial y^2 = 0$. Since CMUI implies constant income elasticities (2.20) reduces to

$$V_{ypp} = \left[\left(\frac{\partial c}{\partial y}\right)^2 - \frac{\partial c}{\partial y \partial p}\right]V_y \ .$$

Thus the effect of price uncertainty on savings depends only on the effect of changes in income on the responsiveness of demand to price and on the absolute value of the income effect. If $\partial c/\partial p$ is constant and $\partial c/\partial y = 0$ savings will be unaffected by price uncertainty. If demand is income responsive in any way while $\partial c/\partial y \partial p = 0$ savings will increase when price variation increases.

Stiglitz [1969] has shown that if preferences are characterized by constant marginal utility of income globally (i.e. if R is constant for all y and p) then the indirect utility function is of the form

$$V(y,p) = a(p)y + b \ .$$

Proposition 2 implies that

$$V_{pp} = a''(p)y > 0$$

indicating $a''(p) > 0$. Hence

$$V_{ypp} = a''(p) > 0 \ .$$

Thus if preferences in period 2 are characterized by global risk neutrality while period 1 preferences are characterized by diminishing marginal utility increased price uncertainty increases optimal savings.

c. Constant Relative Risk Aversion

If the degree of relative risk aversion is unaffected by changes in money income then

$$d(-yV_{yy}/V_y)/dy = 0 \tag{2.21}$$

or

$$V_{yyy} = V_{yy}^2/V_y - V_{yy}/y \; .$$

Substituting equation (2.21) into expression (2.20) yields an expression with the same sign as

$$\left[\partial\left(c\frac{\partial c}{\partial y} - \frac{\partial c}{\partial p}\right)\Big/\partial y\right]\left(\frac{y}{c}\right)^2 + (1 - Z_p - 3Z_y)R + R^2 \; . \tag{2.22}$$

The third term is positive while the second is negative unless the demand for commodity 2 is highly price and income inelastic. The expression is unambiguously positive for very large values of R.

Stiglitz [1969] has shown that if the degree of relative risk aversion is constant for all values of income and prices then demand functions are of the firm

$$c = g(p)y \; .$$

In this case expression (2.22) has the sign of

$$(1-R)\left[Z_p + \frac{c}{y}(1-R)\right] \tag{2.22'}$$

which is positive for $R < 1$, negative for $1 < R < 1 + (y/c)Z_p$, and positive again for $R > 1 + (y/c)Z_p$.

When the degree of relative risk aversion is either very small or very large increased relative price uncertainty increases the expected marginal utility of income in period 2 at a given level of savings. When risk aversion is less than one the increase in the marginal utility of income is caused by the increased flexibility or opportunities for advantageous substitution at the margin afforded by increased price uncertainty. When risk aversion is very great the increase in the expected marginal utility of income is due to the increase in real income variation caused by price uncertainty. In either case the appropriate response is increased savings.

For intermediate levels of risk aversion increased price uncertainty may lower the expected marginal utility of income. The inframarginal increased flexibility provided by opportunities for advantageous substitution of expenditure reduces the marginal value of savings when the marginal utility of income is diminishing rapidly. A transfer of resources to consumption in period 1 is appropriate.

d. Constant Absolute Risk Aversion

If the degree of absolute risk aversion is unaffected by changes in money income

$$d(-V_{yy}/V_y)/dy = 0 \tag{2.23}$$

implying

$$V_{yyy} = V_{yy}^2/V_y \ . \tag{2.24}$$

Substituting equation (2.24) into expression (2.20) gives an expression with the sign of

$$\text{(2.25)} \qquad \left[\partial\left(c\frac{\partial c}{\partial y} - \frac{\partial c}{\partial p}\right)\Big/\partial y\right] - \left(3c\,\frac{\partial c}{\partial y} - \frac{\partial c}{\partial p}\right)A + c^2A^2$$

where

$$A \equiv -V_{yy}/V_y \ .$$

the degree of absolute risk aversion.

Less can be said about the sign of each term in expression (2.25) than in the case of constant relative risk aversion but, again, the expression is likely to be positive when the degree of absolute risk aversion is very large.

e. Iso-Elastic-Marginal Utility with Constant Elasticity of Substitution

The utility function of the form

$$\text{(2.26)} \qquad U(x_1, x_2) = \frac{1}{\gamma}(\alpha_1 x_1^{-\rho} + \alpha_2 x_2^{-\rho})^{-\gamma/\rho}$$

is referred to as the IMU-CES utility function. Here ρ is related to the elasticity of substitution between commodity 1 and commodity 2 by the formula

$$\text{(2.27)} \qquad \rho = \frac{1}{\sigma} - 1 \ .$$

Thus for $\sigma = 0$, $\rho = \infty$; $\sigma = 1$, $\rho = 0$; and $\sigma = \infty$, $\rho = -1$. The term $(1-\gamma)$ is the elasticity of marginal utility or Arrow-Pratt measure of relative risk aversion. The indirect utility function corresponding to (2.26) is of the form

$$(2.28) \qquad V(y,p) = \frac{1}{\gamma} y^{\gamma} D^{\gamma/\sigma-1}$$

where $D = (\alpha_1^{\sigma} + \alpha_2^{\sigma} p^{1-\sigma})$. Differentiating expression (2.28) twice with respect to p and once with respect to y yields

$$(2.29) \qquad V_{ypp} = y^{\gamma-1} D^{-2-\gamma/\sigma-1} p^{-2\sigma} \{\gamma[(1+\gamma)\alpha_2^{\sigma} + \sigma\alpha_1^{\sigma} p^{\sigma-1}]\}$$

which has the same sign as the expression in the ellipses. Expression (2.29) is unambiguously positive for $\gamma > 0$ (relative risk aversion less than unity) and unambiguously negative for $-1 < \gamma < 0$. For $\gamma < -1$ $V_{ypp} \gtrless 0$ as

$$\left(\frac{\alpha_1}{\alpha_2}\right)^{\sigma} \lessgtr \frac{-(1+\gamma)}{\sigma} .$$

Increased uncertainty in the price of commodity 2 is more likely to increase savings (a) the larger α_2 relative to α_1 , or the greater the weight of commodity 2 consumption in utility, (b) the greater $1-\gamma$, the degree of relative risk aversion, and (c) the smaller σ, the elasticity of substitution in consumption.

The effect of the elasticity of substitution, σ , on the responsiveness of expected utility to increased price variation is illustrated in Figure 2.1. Observe that, in Figure 2.1a, where the indifference curves are highly concave to the origin implying a low elasticity of substitution, that the indifference curve attainable at an intermediate price level $\bar{p}$ lies approximately halfway between that attainable at $p_1 < \bar{p}$ and at $p_2 > \bar{p}$ where $\frac{1}{2}p_1 + \frac{1}{2}p_2 = \bar{p}$. In Figure 2.1b, where the degree of concavity is much less and σ consequently much greater, the indif-

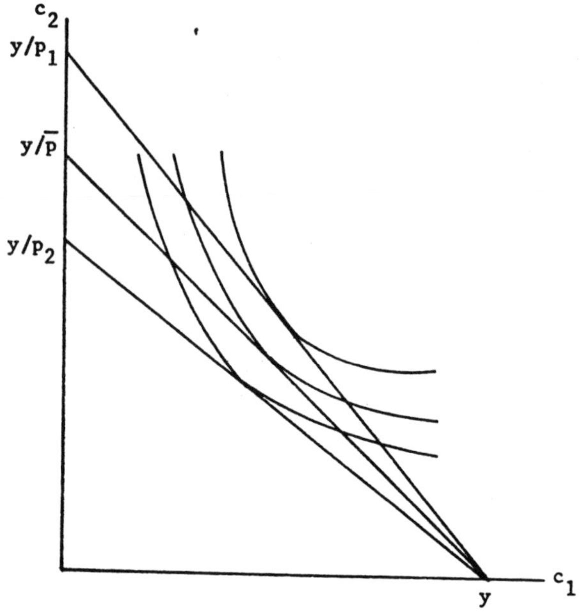

FIGURE 2.1a

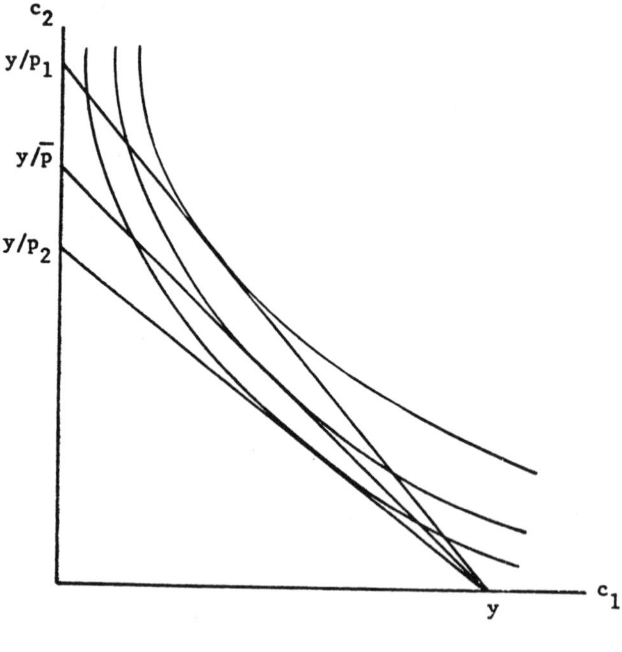

FIGURE 2.1b

ference curve corresponding to $\bar{p}$ lies much closer to that for p_2 than for p_1 : the adverse effect of a high price is relatively less than the beneficial effect of a low price when the elasticity of substitution is large.

For the special case of $\sigma = 1$

$$(2.30) \qquad U(x_1, x_2) = \frac{1}{\gamma}(x_1^{1-\beta} x_2^{\beta})^{\gamma}$$

$$(2.31) \qquad V(y,p) = \frac{1}{\gamma} y^{\gamma} p^{-\beta\gamma}$$

$$(2.32) \qquad V_{ypp} = \beta\gamma(\beta\gamma + 1) y^{\gamma-1} p^{-\beta\gamma-2}$$

which is positive for $\gamma > 0$ or $\gamma < -1/\beta$ and negative for $0 > \gamma > -1/\beta$.

3. The Mean Utility Preserving Increase in Risk

Diamond and Stiglitz [1974] prove that a mean-utility preserving increase in risk increases or decreases the optimal value of a control variable α^* as

$$(2.33) \qquad \frac{V_\theta V_{\alpha\theta\theta} - V_{\alpha\theta} V_{\theta\theta}}{V_\theta} \gtrless 0$$

where $V(\alpha, \theta)$ is the objective function and θ is a random variable of compact support.

If the distribution $F(p)$ is changed to a distribution $G(p)$ such that (1) expected utility is constant and (2) utility is more variable then the effect on optimal savings will be of the same sign as

$$(2.34) \qquad V_{yp}V_{pp} - V_pV_{ypp} = \left[\left(\frac{\partial c}{\partial y}\right)\left(\frac{\partial c}{\partial p}\right) + c^2\frac{\partial^2 c}{\partial y^2} - c\frac{\partial^2 c}{\partial y \partial p}\right]c^2\frac{\partial c}{\partial y}\left(\frac{V_{yy}}{V_y}\right) + c^3\left[\frac{V_{yyy}}{V_y} - \left(\frac{V_{yy}}{V_y}\right)^2\right].$$

In general the sign of the first term is ambiguous. If the income elasticity of demand for commodity 2 is positive the second term is negative while decreasing absolute risk aversion implies a positive third term.

When the utility function is homothetic, i.e. when

$$V(y,p) = f(y)g(p)$$

expression (2.34) reduces to zero. Homotheticity implies that the inframarginal effect of increased price uncertainty, increasing opportunities for advantageous substitution and decreasing optimal savings, exactly offsets the marginal effect, increasing the utility of additional savings when utility is held constant. We conclude

Proposition 3. Homotheticity of the utility function implies that an expected-utility-preserving spread in the distribution of a relative price leaves optimal savings unaffected.[5]

[5] Stiglitz [1969] shows that global constant relative risk aversion and global constant, positive, absolute risk aversion both imply homotheticity.

B. Intertemporally Additively-Inseparable Utility

The assumption of intertemporally additively-separable utility is frequent in economic model building. It is a highly convenient one in that standard techniques such as dynamic programming and optimal control are enormously simplified when the objective function is expressable as the sum or integral over time of intermediate functions whose arguments depend only on contemporaneous values of state and control variables. (See Intriligator [1971], for instance.) In the multi-commodity case intertemporal additive separability implies that the marginal utility of consumption of any commodity in any period does not depend on the level of consumption of any commodity in any other period. This removes from the analysis any question of the intertemporal substitutability of commodities. As an alternative one might hypothesize that a change in consumption of commodity i in period t will affect the marginal utility of consumption of commodity j in period $t+h$, $h \neq 0$. Food might represent a commodity for which the degree of intertemporal substitution is low while recreation may be subject to great intertemporal substitutability. Commodities which are "habit-forming" may be considered intertemporally complementary.[6]

The general form of the *ex post* utility function when there is only a single riskless asset and two commodities is

$$(2.35) \qquad V(c_1^1,\ c_2^1,\ y^1 + y^2 - c_1^1 - c_2^1,\ p)\ .$$

[6] The relationship between saving and uncertainty when there is a single physical commodity in each period and utility is not intertemporally additively separable has been analyzed by Kihlstrom and Mirman [1974].

In period one c_1^1 and c_2^1 are chosen to maximize the expected value of (2.35).

It is convenient to assume that the direct utility function may be written as

$$(2.36) \qquad U[u^1(c^1), u^2(c^2)]$$

in which case the composition of period 1 expenditure on commodities is independent of the optimal composition of period 2 consumption expenditure.

When the direct utility function is of the form of (2.36) one may treat period 1 consumption as a Hicks' composite commodity since the first-order conditions for the optimal allocation of period 2 consumption depends only on $y^2 + s$ and period 2 prices. Similarly the optimal allocation of consumption in period 1 depends only on $y^1 - s$ and prices in period 1.

It is simple to show that, if the form of the direct utility function in expression (2.36) is assumed, then the ex post utility function may be written as

$$(2.37) \qquad U[V^1(y^1 - s), V^2(y^2 + s, p)] .$$

It is assumed that conditions on the direct utility function (2.36) guarantee that $V_y^2 > 0$, $V_{yy}^2 \leq 0$, $U' > 0$, and $U'' < 0$. V^1 is referred to as period 1 utility and V^2 as period 2 utility. Three different forms of the function U are examined.

1. Zero Elasticity of Substitution

If (2.37) is of the form

$$(2.37a) \qquad U = \min[V^1(y^1 - s), V^2(y^2 + s, p)]$$

and if the initial situation is one of certainty then a first-order condition for a maximum is

$$(2.38) \qquad V^1(y^1 - s) = V^2(y^2 + s,\ p)\ ;$$

savings will be allocated so that utility in period 2 is the same as utility in period 1. If this condition is not met utility can always be increased by transferring consumption to the period of lower utility.

When the elasticity of substitution between period 1 and period 2 utility is zero introducing price uncertainty will increase or decrease savings as

$$(2.39) \qquad V^2_{pp} \lessgtr 0\ .$$

When price uncertainty raises utility in period 2 optimal behavior involves transferring savings to period 1 consumption and conversely.

2. Unit Elasticity of Substitution

Consider a function U of the form

$$(2.37b) \qquad [V^1(y_1 - s)]^{\alpha}[V^2(y^2 + s,\ p)]^{\beta}\ .$$

Homotheticity of u^2 in (2.36) implies

$$V^2(y^2 + s,\ p) = m(y^2 + s)c(p)$$

and expression (2.37) may be written

$$(2.37b') \qquad U = [V^1(y_1 - s)]^{\alpha}[m(y^2 + s)]^{\beta}[c(p)]^{\beta}\ .$$

The first-order condition for an optimal value of s is

$$E\{-\alpha V_y^1(y_1 - s)[V^1(y_1^{'} - s)]^{-1}U + \beta m'(y^2 + s)[m(y^2 + s)]^{-1}U\} = 0 \; . \tag{2.40}$$

The term E(U) may be factored out leaving a first-order condition independent of the random variable p .

One may conclude that, when the period 2 utility function is homothetic and the elasticity of substitution between period 1 and period 2 utility is 1 increased price uncertainty does not affect optimal savings.

3. Infinite Elasticity of Substitution

Now consider the function U to be of the form

$$U[V^1(y^1 - s) + V^2(y^2 + s, \; p)] \; . \tag{2.37c}$$

Part A considers the special case in which U is linear.

The first-order condition for an optimal value of s is given by

$$E\{U'[-V_y^1 + V_y^2]\} = 0 \; . \tag{2.41}$$

The effect of increased relative price uncertainty on optimal savings has the sign of

$$U'V_{ypp}^2 + 2U''V_{yp}^2V_p^2 + (-V_y^1 + V_y^2)[U''V_{pp}^2 + U'''(V_p^2)^2] \; . \tag{2.42}$$

If the initial situation is one of certainty the deviation from the optimality condition under certainty

$$-V_y^1 + V_y^2 = 0$$

remains small. In this case the last term may be ignored.

Expression (2.42) exceeds the term V^2_{ypp} , the condition when U is linear, by an amount with sign

(2.43) $A(R_2 - Z_y)$

where

$$R_2 = -yV^2_{yy}/V^2_y$$

and

$$A = -U''/U' .$$

On one hand, increased savings transfers expenditure from safe period 1 consumption to risky period 2 consumption. Lower savings thus reduces the riskiness of expenditure over the two periods. On the other hand when period 2 utility is a diminishing function of consumption expenditures in period 2 a given level of price uncertainty at a given level of consumption of commodity 2 creates a greater amount of uncertainty in period 2 utility when consumption expenditure is low. The first effect lowers optimal savings when price uncertainty increases while the second tends to raise savings.

If

(2.44) $u^2(c^2_1, c^2_2) = c^{2\,1-\beta}_1 c^{2\,\beta}_2$

and if the initial situation is one of certainty then expression (2.42) has the same sign as

(2.45) $1 + \beta[1 - 2RV^2/(V^1 + V^2)]$

where

$$R \equiv -U''(V^1 + V^2)/U' \ .$$

If the degree of overall risk aversion, R, and the share of period 2 utility in total utility is large, increased price uncertainty is likely to reduce savings. In this case the safer period 1 income is preferred. When the degree of risk-aversion is smaller the increased flexibility of period 2 expenditure increases savings.

C. Stochastic Income, Rate of Return and Relative Price

Parts A and B considered the effect on savings of an increase in the uncertainty of the relative price of commodity 2 in an environment in which y^2, second period income, and r, the rate of return on savings, in terms of commodity 1's price are non-random. This section considers the effect of relative price uncertainty in a more general stochastic environment.

The Rothschild-Stiglitz criterion for determining the effect of increased risk on the value of a control variable does not generalize in a helpful way to the case in which more than one variable is stochastic. The alternative approach adopted is the treatment of $E[V_y]$ in terms of a second-order Taylor series expansion around $y^2 = \bar{y}$, $r = \bar{r}$, and $p = \bar{p}$. While this approach yields good approximations for $f(y,r,p)$ with small higher-order moments it provides an exact depiction of $E[V_y]$ if the movements of y, r, and p are characterized by discrete-time Wiener processes of the form

$$\text{(2.46)} \qquad \begin{aligned} p &= 1 + \\ r &= \bar{r} + F \\ y^2 &= y^1 + \end{aligned} \begin{bmatrix} z_p \\ z_r \\ z_y \end{bmatrix}$$

where

$$F'F = \begin{bmatrix} \sigma_p^2 & \sigma_{pr} & \sigma_{py} \\ \sigma_{pr} & \sigma_r^2 & \sigma_{ry} \\ \sigma_{py} & \sigma_{ry} & \sigma_y^2 \end{bmatrix},$$

the variance-covariance matrix of the processes, and $z_i \sim N(0,1)$, $i = p, r, y^2$.

The individual saves to equate

$$(2.47) \qquad V_y^1 = E[rV_y^2] \ .$$

Expanding the right side of (2.47) yields

$$(2.48) \ E[rV_y^2(y^2, r, p)] = \bar{r}V_y^2(\bar{y}, \bar{r}, 1) + V_y s\sigma_r + \bar{r}[\tfrac{1}{2}V_{yyy}(\sigma_y^2 + \sigma_r^2 s^2 + \rho_{ry}\sigma_r\sigma_y s) + V_{yyp}\sigma_p\lambda + \tfrac{1}{2}V_{ypp}\sigma_p^2]$$

where $\lambda = (\rho_{py}\sigma_y + \sigma_{pr}\sigma_r s)$ and $s = y^1 - c^1$ first period savings. The direction of the effect of increased relative price uncertainty on optimal savings (as measured by an increase in the variance of the Wiener process, σ_p) is given by the sign of

$$(2.49) \qquad \frac{1}{\bar{r}}\frac{\partial V_y^2}{\partial \sigma_p} = V_{yyp}\lambda + V_{ypp}\sigma_p \ .$$

Expression (2.49) may be written as

$$(2.50)\sigma_p\left\{\left[\frac{\partial^2 c}{\partial y^2}(c - \lambda') + \frac{\partial^2 c}{\partial y^2} - \frac{\partial c}{\partial y \partial p}\right]V_y + \left[\frac{\partial c}{\partial y}(3c - 2\lambda') - \frac{\partial c}{\partial p}\right]V_{yy} + c(c - \lambda\gamma)V_{yyy}\right\}$$

where $\lambda' = \lambda/\sigma_p$. If $\lambda > 0$ the relative price of commodity 2 is positively correlated with capital and non-capital income in period 2. This will tend to diminish the income effect of price uncertainty when $c > 0$ and augment it for $c < 0$. Conversely for $\lambda < 0$.

In the case of the IMU-CES utility function discussed in Part A

$$(2.51) \qquad V_{yyp} = \gamma(1-\gamma)y^{\gamma-2}(\alpha_1' + \alpha_2' p^{\rho/1+\rho})^{[-\gamma(1+\rho)/\rho]-1} p^{-1/1+\rho}$$

which is positive for $\gamma < 0$ and negative for $\gamma > 0$. Combining (2.51) with (2.29) we note that if $\lambda < 0$ (the price of commodity 2 is negatively correlated with income) increased price variability is unambiguously associated with increased savings for $1 > \gamma > 0$ and with decreased savings for $0 > \gamma > -1$. For $\gamma < -1$ a negative relationship between savings and price uncertainty will obtain at higher levels of ρ (lower elasticities of substitution) than when $\lambda = 0$.

III. Relative Price Uncertainty and Savings with Multiple Assets: Two-Period Analysis

Sections I and II have considered the effect of changes in the subjective probability distribution of future relative prices on welfare and savings when only one asset, with rate of return uncertain either in terms of commodity 2 or in terms of both prices, is available. This section discusses the effect of relative price uncertainty on welfare, savings and portfolio behavior when there exists for each price an asset with rate of return equal to the rate of change of that price. These assets may be thought of as shares in firms producing the commodity in question, or as inventories or forward purchases of the commodity itself. This section treats (1) the determinants of demand for each asset, (2) the effect of increased price uncertainty on expected utility and (3) the relationship between savings and relative price uncertainty when such assets are available.

Asset 1 has a rate of return equal to the rate of price increase of commodity 1 while asset 2's rate of return is commodity 2's rate of price increase. The share of savings held in asset 2 is denoted by ω .

In terms of the *ex post* utility function, expression (2.3), the objective function is

$$E\{V[c_1^1,\ c_2^1,\ y^2 + (y^1 - c_1^1 - c_2^1)(1 - \omega + p\omega),\ p]\} . \tag{3.1}$$

In Part A the case in which the direct utility function is intertemporally additively separable is considered while in Part B this assumption is relaxed.

A. Intertemporally-Additively Separable Utility

If the direct utility function is of the form

$$(3.2)\qquad U^1(c_1^1, c_2^1) + U^2(c_1^2, c_2^2)$$

period 1 consumption may be treated as a Hicks' composite commodity and the *ex post* utility function may be written as

$$(3.3)\qquad V^1(y^1 - s) + V^2[y^2 + s(1 - \omega + p\omega), p] .$$

The consumer chooses s and ω to maximize the expected value of (3.3). First-order conditions for a maximum are

$$(3.4a)\qquad E[V_y^1 + (1 - \omega + p\omega)V_y^2] = 0$$

$$(3.4b)\qquad E[(p-1)sV_y^2] = 0 .$$

Concavity of V^2 in y guarantees that the second-order conditions for a maximum are satisfied.

The analysis is limited to the case in which the only source of uncertainty is the variable p ; y^2 is known with certainty. It is convenient to depart from the analysis of changes in general distribution functions and make a specific assumption about the distribution of p . Assume that price variation is generated by a discrete-time Wiener process

$$(3.5)\qquad p = \bar{p}(1 + \sigma z) , \quad z \sim N(0,1) .$$

With this assumption expected utility is equal to

$$(3.6) \qquad E(u) = V^1(y^1 - s) + V^2[y^2 + s(1 - \omega + \omega\bar{p}), \bar{p}] + (\frac{1}{2}V_{pp} + s\omega V_{yp} + \frac{1}{2}s^2\omega^2 V_{yy})\sigma^2 .$$

The first-order condition for an optimal value of ω, given s, is given by

$$(3.7) \qquad s(\bar{p}-1)[V_y + (\frac{1}{2}V_{ypp} + s\omega V_{yyp} + \frac{1}{2}s^2\omega^2 V_{yyy})\sigma_p^2] + (sV_{yp} + s^2\omega V_{yy})\sigma_p^2 = 0 .$$

If there is no expected change in the price of commodity 2 $\bar{p} = 1$ and

$$(3.8) \qquad s^*\omega^* = -\frac{V_{yp}}{V_{yy}} = \left[\frac{\partial c}{\partial y}\frac{V_y}{V_{yy}} + c\right]$$

where s^* and ω^* represent optimal savings and the optimal share of savings held in asset 2, respectively.

Expression (3.8) implies that optimal holdings of asset 2 are equal to

$$(3.9) \qquad s^*\omega^* = c(R - Z_y)/R$$

where

$$R = -yV_{yy}/V_y$$

the degree of relative risk aversion and

$$Z_y = \frac{\partial c}{\partial y}\frac{y}{c}$$

the income-elasticity of demand for commodity 2. If $Z_y > R$ the fact that holding asset 2 at positive levels introduces a positive correlation between income and price makes negative holdings of asset 2 optimal. When $Z_y < R$ risk aversion leads to positive holdings of asset 2. One may conclude:

<u>Proposition 4</u>. Holdings of the asset with rate of return equal to the rate of change of the uncertain prices are positive or negative as the degree of relative risk aversion exceeds or is less than the income elasticity of demand for the commodity with uncertain price.

Expression (3.8) indicates:

<u>Proposition 5</u>. Optimal holdings of asset 2 are independent of the price variance.

and

<u>Proposition 6</u>. If $-V_{yy}/V_y = \infty$ (extreme risk aversion) or $\partial c/\partial y = 0$ (zero income elasticity of demand for commodity 2), $s^*\omega^* = c$: demand for asset 2 equals demand for commodity 2. If there is positive income elasticity of demand for commodity 2 or less than infinite risk aversion $s^*\omega^* < c$ and if $\partial c/\partial y < 0$, $s^*\omega^* > c$.

When commodity 2 is non-inferior the consumer speculates by not insuring fully against price uncertainty. If it is inferior he overinsures.

Substituting expression (3.8), optimal demand for asset 2, into the expression (3.6) for expected utility gives

$$(3.10) \qquad E(u) = V^1(y^1 - s) + V^2(y^2 + s,\ 1) + \tfrac{1}{2}[V_{pp}^2 - (V_{yp}^2)^2/V_{yy}^2]\sigma^2 .$$

The coefficient of σ^2 in expression (3.10) is equal to

$$(3.11) \qquad \frac{1}{2}V_y\left[-\left(\frac{\partial c}{\partial y}\right)^2 V_y/V_{yy} + 3c\left(\frac{\partial c}{\partial y}\right) - \frac{\partial c}{\partial p}\right]$$

$$= \frac{1}{2}V_y(c^2/y)\left[\frac{Z_y^2}{R} + 3Z_y + Z_p\left(\frac{y}{c}\right)\right]$$

which is always positive when $Z_y > 0$. This result demonstrates

Proposition 7. Increased variance in the price of a commodity with positive income elasticity of demand always increases expected utility when an asset is available with rate of return equal to the rate of price change. The increase in expected utility caused by a given increase in variance is greater the greater the share of the consumption of the commodity in expenditure, the greater the price and income elasticities of demand for the commodity, and the lower the degree of relative risk aversion.

The availability of asset 2 allows the household to offset the income effect of increased variance in the price of commodity 2. The opportunities for increased substitution in response to price movements nevertheless remain as long as $Z_y \neq 0$ or $Z_p \neq 0$.

The effect of increased variance in the price of commodity 2 on savings is obtained by differentiating expression (3.10) with respect to s . This gives as a first-order condition for a maximum

$$(3.12) \qquad -V_y^1 + V_y^2 + \sigma^2\left\{\frac{1}{2}V_{ypp}^2 - \frac{V_{yp}^2 V_{yyp}^2}{V_{yy}^2} + \frac{(V_{yp}^2)^2 V_{yyy}^2}{2(V_{yy}^2)^2}\right\} \quad .$$

The coefficient of the variance has the same sign as

$$(3.13) \qquad (1-R)[RZ_p + \frac{c}{y}(1-R)]$$

which is positive for $R < 1$ and negative for $R > 1$ if $Z_p > c/y$. If $Z_p < c/y$ then expression (3.13) becomes positive again when $R > 1/[1 - (y/c)Z_p]$. The more risk averse (those with $R > 1$) always decrease savings when the increase in relative price uncertainty applies to a commodity with price elasticity of demand greater than its share in expenditure. If demand for the commodity is price inelastic the very risk averse may increase savings in response to increased uncertainty nevertheless.

Comparing expression (3.13) with expression (2.22') above one observes that, when a second asset is available, the range of values of the degree of risk aversion generating a negative response in savings to increased price uncertainty is increased. Even the extremely risk averse may reduce savings in response to increased price uncertainty when a second asset is available. When the degree of relative risk aversion is very high the income effect of increased price uncertainty operates to increase savings when there is only a single asset. When asset 2 is available, however, the real income variation generated by relative price variation disappears as holdings of asset 2 approach the level of consumption of commodity 2.

B. Intertemporally-Additively Inseparable Utility

The general expression for the *ex post* utility function for the two-asset, two-commodity case is given in expression (3.1). Again assume that the direct utility function is expressible in the form of (2.36) above. One may then treat period 1 consumption as a Hicks' composite commodity and write the *ex post* utility function as

$$(3.14) \qquad U\{V^1(y^1 - s),\ V^2[y^2 + s(1 - \omega + p\omega),\ p]\}\ .$$

As before, assume that conditions on the direct utility function guarantee that $V_y^2 > 0$, $V_{yy}^2 \leq 0$, $U' > 0$ and $U'' < 0$.

The cases of zero, unit and infinite elasticities of substitution between utility in each period are again considered.

1. Zero Elasticity of Substitution

If the indirect utility function is of the form

$$(3.14a) \qquad U = \min[V^1(y^1 - s),\ V^2(y^2 + s,\ p)]$$

and the initial situation is one of certainty then optimality requires that

$$(3.15) \qquad V^1(y^1 - s) = V^2(y^2 + s,\ p)\ .$$

The effect of introducing price uncertainty on optimal savings then depends on the sign of $-V_{pp}$. Proposition 7 states that when price movement is characterized by a discrete-time Wiener process increased price variation increases expected utility in period 2 if there are assets for each commodity. One may conclude, therefore, that introducing price uncertainty will lower optimal savings when the objective function is of the form of (3.14a) and price changes are normally distributed.

2. Unit Elasticity of Substitution

If the function U is of the form

$$(3.14b) \qquad [V^1(y_1 - s)]^{\alpha}[V^2(y^2 + s(1 - \omega + p\omega), p]^{\beta}$$

and if the function h in expression (2.38) is homothetic one may write the objective function as

$$E\{[V^1(y_1 - s)]^{\alpha} [m(y^2 + s(1 - \omega + p\omega))]^{\beta} [c(p)]^{\beta}\} .$$

The first-order condition for an optimal value of s is

$$(3.16) \qquad E\{U[-\alpha V^1 y(V^1)^{-1} + \beta m' m^{-1}(1 - \omega + p\omega)]\}$$

The determinants of the effect of increased price uncertainty on optimal savings are difficult to ascertain. It is clear from expression (3.16), however, that optimal savings is not independent of the price distribution as it is in the one-asset case. Price uncertainty introduces uncertainty in the level of money expenditure in period 2 as well as in relative prices. Only if $y^2 = 0$ and $m'' = 0$ does the independence of optimal savings from the price distribution obtain. In this case price uncertainty is proportional to uncertainty in the utility of expenditure in period 2 and optimal intertemporal allocation of expenditure is indicated by the shares α and β only.

3. Infinite Elasticity of Substitution

If the function U is of the form

$$(3.14c) \qquad U[V^1(y^1 - s) + V^2(y^2 + s(1 - \omega + p\omega), p)]$$

the first-order condition for a maximum is given by

(3.17) $$E\{U'[-V_y^1 + V_y^2]\} = 0 .$$

It is assumed, as before, that the range of variation of p is small. In this case the expression for $d^2[U'(-V_y^1 + V_y^2)]/dp^2$ exceeds that for the case in which $U'' = 0$ by an amount with the sign of

(3.18) $$A(c - s\omega)\left[\left(\frac{c - s\omega}{c}\right) R_2 - Z_y\right]$$

where

$$A = -U''/U'$$

$$R_2 = -yV_{yy}^2/V_y^2$$

and

$$Z_y = \frac{\partial c}{\partial y}\frac{y}{c} .$$

If $c > s\omega$, then expression (3.18) has the same sign as

(3.19) $$A\left[\left(\frac{c - s\omega}{c}\right) R_2 - Z_y\right]$$

which is negative unless "unhedged" purchases of commodity 2 are large relative to total commodity 2 purchases and the degree of risk aversion is large while the income elasticity of demand is small.

Comparing expression (3.18) with its counterpart for the one asset case,

(2.43) $$A(R_2 - Z_y)$$

one observes that, in the two-asset case, savings is more likely to drop as A changes from 0 to a positive number. An increase in the sum of utilities in the two periods can now better be accomplished by consuming safely in period 1 since the income effect of price uncertainty on the marginal utility of period 2 income may be offset by holdings of asset 2.

IV. Multiperiod Analysis

Sections II and III considered optimal savings and portfolio behavior in a two-period context. The two-period analysis is appropriate to situations in which the period 2 price, once realized, is expected to remain stable. This is clearly more descriptive of situations where price uncertainty is generated by once and for all changes in market conditions, such as forthcoming deregulation or cartel formation, than others, such as price uncertainty generated by technological uncertainty or weather, for instance.

This section discusses, under two separate assumptions about dynamic stochastic price behavior, considerations affecting optimal savings in a multiperiod context. First introduced is a discrete-time formulation of savings and relative price behavior to analyze the effect of increased price uncertainty in a particular period on savings in previous periods, holding the price distributions in all other periods constant. Secondly, in a continuous-time formulation, the effect of increasing "white noise" in price variation on optimal savings is derived. Here the increase in uncertainty applies to all remaining periods.

It is assumed throughout this section that the direct and hence indirect utility functions are intertemporally additively separable.

A. Discrete-Time Analysis

The consumer seeks to maximize the sum of expected utility over T periods

$$(4.1) \qquad E[\sum_{i=1}^{T} V^i(c^i, p^i)]$$

where p^i represents the relative price of commodity 2 in period i and c^i consumption expenditures in period i. The consumer earns an income y^i in period i and saves $s^i = y^i + s^{i-1} - c^i$ where s^{i-1} represents savings in the preceding period.

The subjective probability density function of p^i is given by

$$(4.2) \qquad f^i(p^i | p^{i-1}, \ldots, p^1)$$

which is assumed to be of compact support. If the p^i are independently distributed then

$$(4.3) \qquad f^i(p^i | p^{i-1}, \ldots, p^1) = f^i(p^i) , \quad i = 1, \ldots, T .$$

To obtain a first-order condition for optimal savings in period i the objective function may be written

$$(4.1') \qquad E[\sum_{i=1}^{T} V^i(y^i + s^{i-1} - s^i, p^i)]$$

and differentiated with respect to s^i, to obtain

$$(4.4) \; -V_y^i(y^i + s^{i-1} - s^i, p^i) + \int V_y^{i+1}(y^{i+1} + s^i - s^{i+1}, p^{i+1}) f(p^{i+1} | p^i \ldots) .$$

Expression (4.4) implicitly defines a function for optimal savings in period

i in terms of savings in period $i-1$, and price in period i:

$$s^i = s^i(s^{i-1}, p^i) . \tag{4.5}$$

By appropriate differentiation of expression (4.4) one may observe that

$$1 \geq \frac{ds^i}{ds^{i-1}} = \frac{V^i_{yy}}{V^i_{yy} + E[V^{i+1}_{yy}]} \geq 0 . \tag{4.6}$$

Savings in period i is an increasing function of savings in period $i-1$. When the p^i are independently distributed

$$\frac{ds^i}{dp^i} = \frac{V^i_{yp}}{V^i_{yy} + E[V^{i+1}_{yy}]} \tag{4.7}$$

which has the same sign as $Z_y - R$. If the degree of relative risk aversion is larger than the income elasticity of demand for commodity 2 savings is lower when p^i is higher: when the marginal utility of income diminishes rapidly the consumer is less willing to postpone consumption until "better times." If the income elasticity of demand for commodity 2 is large savings reduces the effect of a high price in period i.

The effect of increased price uncertainty in period i on expected utility and on optimal savings in previous periods may now be analyzed. By applying Theorem 1 of the first essay it can be shown that when prices are independently distributed increased price uncertainty in period i increases or decreases expected utility as

$$-V^i_{yp}\left(\frac{ds^i}{dp}\right) + V^i_{pp} \gtrless 0 . \tag{4.8}$$

The first term is always nonnegative. Increased price uncertainty in one period is less likely to reduce expected utility in a multiperiod context. Savings in period i represents an introduction of an additional *ex post* control. The consumer may offset the effect of price changes by transferring expenditure into or out of the period in which price uncertainty is increasing.

If the marginal utility of income in period $i+1$ is constant expression (4.8) is always positive: by transferring expenditure into or away from consumption in period i the consumer can always increase expected utility no matter how risk-averse he is with respect to period i income.

The effect of a mean-preserving spread in the distribution of p^i on savings in period $i-1$ is given by the sign of

$$(4.9) \qquad -V^i_{yy}(d^2s^i/dp^{i^2}) + V^i_{yyy}(ds^{i+1}/dp^i)^2 - 2V^i_{yyp}(ds^i/dp^i) + V^i_{ypp} \, .$$

Only if $ds^i/dp^i = 0$ does condition (4.9) reduce to the expression obtained in the two-period case. Increased uncertainty in a multiperiod context does not in general have the same effect on optimal savings as in the two-period model.

B. Continuous-Time Analysis

In Part A the effect on welfare and savings of increasing price uncertainty in one period holding the price distributions in other periods was explored. If the source of increased uncertainty is short term, such as unusual weather conditions in one growing season, this model is appropriate. If, however, a structural change occurs, such as deregulation or decartelization, permanently increasing price uncertainty an alternative model is more descriptive.

In this section a life-cycle model of optimal consumption is developed in which the movement of the relative price of a commodity is characterized by a continuous-time Wiener process. The comparative dynamics of increased uncertainty in this context may be treated by analyzing the effect of increasing the coefficient of the random part of the Wiener process.

Both the one-asset and multi-asset cases are treated. Intertemporal additive separability of utility is assumed throughout.

1. The One-Asset Case

The individual seeks to maximize lifetime utility and a bequest function

$$\int_0^T V(c(t),\ p(t))e^{-\delta t}dt + B(W(T),\ p(T)) \tag{4.10}$$

where $W(T)$ represents terminal wealth. Here $c(t)$ represents consumption expenditures in period t, a control variable, and $p(t)$ represents the relative price of commodity 2 at time t. The time rate of discount is δ. The movements of the random variables y, r, and p are characterized as Itô processes of the form

(4.11a) $$\frac{dp}{p} = \alpha_p dt + \sigma_p dz_p$$

(4.11b) $$dr = \alpha_r dt + \sigma_r dz_r$$

(4.11c) $$dy = \alpha_y dt + \sigma_y dz_y \ .$$

Here the dz_i represent independent Wiener processes for which

$$\sigma_i dz_i(t) = \lim_{h \to 0} \sigma_i(h) a_i(h)\sqrt{h}$$

where $a_i(t) \sim N(0,1)$ and $\mathrm{var}(a_i(t), a_i(t+\epsilon)) = 0$ for $\epsilon \neq 0$.[7] The correlation coefficients of the $a_i(t)$ are given by ρ_{ij} . Here dy may be interpreted as the instantaneous flow of non-capital income while dr represents the instantaneous flow of capital income per unit of capital.

The change in wealth at each moment is given by the stochastic differential equation

(4.12) $$dW = [dy - c dt + W dr] = [\alpha_y - c + \alpha_r W]dt + \sigma_y dz_y + \sigma_r W dz_r \ .$$

---

[7] It can be shown (see Fischer [1975]) that (4.11a) implies that variable p(t) has log-normal distribution with

$$E[\log \frac{p(t)}{p(0)}] = (\alpha_p - \frac{\sigma_p^2}{2})t \quad \text{and}$$

$$\mathrm{var}[\log \frac{p(t)}{p(0)}] = \sigma^2 t \ .$$

Let $J(W(t), p(t), t)$ represent the expected discounted value of consumption between time t and T plus the utility attached to bequested wealth

$$(4.13) \qquad J(W(t), p(t), t) = \max_{c(\tau)} E[\int_t^T V(c(\tau), p(\tau), \tau)d\tau + B(W(T), p(T)].$$

Applying the continuous-time version of the Bellman-Dreyfus fundamental equation of optimality yields

$$(4.14) \qquad J(t) = E[\int_t^{t+h} V(c^*(\tau), p(\tau))e^{-\delta\tau}d\tau + e^{-\delta(t+h)}J(t+h)]$$

which, in the limit as $h \to 0$ becomes

$$(4.15) \qquad V(c^*(t), p(t))e^{-\delta t} + \lim_{h\to 0}\left[\frac{e^{-\delta(t+h)}J(t+h) - J(t)}{h}\right] = 0$$

where $c^*(\tau)$ represents optimal consumption at time τ.[8] The second term of (4.15) may be evaluated by application of the Dynkin operator to the function J over the stochastic variables W and p for given c. This yields:

$$(4.16) \qquad V(c^*(t), p(t))e^{-\delta t} + J_t + J_w[dy - c + \alpha_r W] + J_p\alpha_p p + \tfrac{1}{2}J_{pp}\sigma_p^2 p^2$$
$$+ \tfrac{1}{2}J_{ww}[\sigma_r^2 W^2 + \sigma_y^2 + \rho_{ry}\sigma_r\sigma_y W] + J_{pw}\sigma_p p[\rho_{pr}\sigma_r W + \rho_{py}\sigma_y] .$$

The first-order condition for a maximum is found by differentiating (4.16) w.r.t. c yielding

[8] Concavity of V in c and B in W guarantees satisfaction of the second-order conditions for a maximum.

$$(4.17) \qquad V_y(c^*(t), p(t), t) - J_w(W(t), p(t), t) = 0 .$$

At each instant the individual consumes up to the point at which the marginal utility of present consumption equals the contribution of a marginal unit of wealth to expected discounted future utility.

Condition (4.17) together with the optimality condition (4.16) and the boundary condition

$$(4.18) \qquad J[W(T), p(T), T] = B[W(T), p(T)]$$

define an optimal value of $c^*(t)$ as a function of $W(t)$, $p(t)$, and t. Differentiating (4.17) with respect to W yields

$$(4.19) \qquad V_{yy} \frac{\partial c^*}{\partial W} = J_{WW}$$

which, by concavity of V in y and J in W, implies $\partial c^*/\partial W > 0$. Similarly, differentiation of (4.17) with respect to p yields

$$(4.20) \qquad V_{yy} \frac{\partial c^*}{\partial p} + V_{yp} = J_{wp}$$

implying

$$(4.21) \qquad \frac{\partial c^*}{\partial p} = \frac{1}{V_{yy}}(J_{wp} + \frac{\partial c}{\partial y} V_y) + c$$

which is of indeterminate sign.

The system defined by conditions (4.16), (4.17), and (4.18) is, in general, difficult to solve and comparative static and dynamic results are of indeterminate sign. For particular forms of the utility function, however, explicit solutions are available which yield determinate results. For the utility function of the form

$$(4.22) \qquad U(x_1, x_2, t) = \frac{1}{\gamma}(x_1^{1-\beta} x_2^{\beta})^{\gamma} e^{-\delta t} \quad \text{for} \quad \gamma < 1 \, , \quad 1 > \beta > 0$$

the corresponding indirect utility function is

$$(4.23) \qquad V(c,p,t) = \frac{1}{\gamma} c^{\gamma} p^{-\beta\gamma} e^{-\delta t}$$

which is characterized by constant relative risk aversion (iso-elastic marginal utility).[9] Substituting (4.23) into conditions (4.17) and (4.16) respectively yields

$$(4.24) \qquad c^* = [J_W p^{\beta\gamma} e^{\delta t}]^{1/\gamma - 1}$$

and

$$(4.25) \qquad \left(\frac{1-\gamma}{\gamma}\right)(J_W^{\gamma} p^{\beta\gamma} e^{\delta t})^{1/\gamma - 1} + J_W(\alpha_y + \alpha_r W) + J_p \alpha_p p + \frac{1}{2} J_{WW} \sigma_W^2 + \frac{1}{2} J_{pp} \sigma_p^2 p^2 + J_{Wp} \sigma_p \sigma_W p \; .$$

Ignoring non-wealth income by setting $\alpha_y = \sigma_y = 0$ simplifies the analysis enormously. It is also convenient to assume that the bequest function is

$$(4.26) \qquad B[W(T), p(T), T] = e^{-\delta T} \frac{\mu}{\gamma} W(T)^{\gamma} p(T)^{-\beta\gamma}$$

where $\mu \geq 0$. Consider (4.25) to have a solution of the form

$$(4.27) \qquad J[W(t), p(t), t] = \frac{b(t)}{\gamma} e^{-\delta t} W(t)^{\gamma} p(t)^{-\beta\gamma} \; .$$

Substituting (4.27) into (4.25) yields the differential equation:

[9] A very similar problem, for the one-commodity case, is solved by Merton [1969].

$$(4.28) \qquad \dot{b}(t) = \nu \cdot b(t) + (\gamma-1)b(t)^{\gamma/\gamma-1}$$

where

$$(4.29) \qquad \nu = [\delta + \beta\gamma\alpha_p + \beta\gamma^2\rho_{pr}\sigma_p\sigma_r - \gamma\alpha_r - \tfrac{1}{2}\gamma(\gamma-1)\sigma_r^2 - \tfrac{1}{2}\beta\gamma(\beta\gamma+1)\sigma_p^2]$$

subject to

$$(4.30) \qquad b(T) = \mu \; .$$

The solution to (4.28) with the boundary condition (4.30) is

$$(4.31) \qquad b(t) = \{\epsilon(1 - e^{\epsilon(t-T)}) + \mu^{1/1-\gamma}e^{\epsilon(t-T)}\}^{1-\gamma}$$

where $\epsilon = \nu/1-\gamma$. Note that $b(t) \geq 0$ for all values of ϵ and hence of ν .

Differentiating (4.27) w.r.t. W gives

$$(4.32) \qquad J_w = b(t)W^{\gamma-1}p^{-\beta\gamma}e^{-\delta t}$$

which, when substituted into (4.24) yields

$$(4.33) \qquad c^*(t) = b(t)W(t) \; .$$

In the Cobb-Douglas iso-elastic marginal utility case the optimal level of expenditure in each period is independent of the relative price of commodity 2. Thus, just as a change in relative price does not affect the allocation of expenditure among commodities in a single period in the Cobb-Douglas case it does not affect the allocation of expenditure among time periods.

If $\mu = 0$ or if $T-t$ is very large then $b(t)$ is increasing in ϵ which is in turn an increasing function of ν . From expression

(4.9), if $\rho_{pr} = 0$ then, an increase in σ_p^2 increases or decreases ν as

$$(4.34) \qquad -\beta\gamma(\beta\gamma + 1) \gtrless 1 .$$

This term is negative for $\gamma > 0$ and $\gamma < 1/\beta$ and positive for $0 > \gamma > 1/\beta$: for a given level of wealth increased price uncertainty reduces consumption (raises savings) when the degree of relative risk aversion is less than one or greater than $1 + 1/\beta$. This is equivalent **to the** condition derived in the two-period analysis in Section II. For the Cobb-Douglas case, at least, increased price uncertainty has the same effect on optimal consumption in the two-period and continuous-time models.

2. The Multi-Asset Case

Similar results may be derived for the two-asset model. Modifying the analysis above accordingly, the rate of change of wealth is

$$(4.35) \qquad dW = [dy - cdt + Wdr] = [\alpha_y - c + wW\alpha_p]dt + wW\sigma_p dz_p + \sigma_y dz_y .$$

Substituting (4.35) into the continuous-time version of the Bellman-Dreyfus optimality condition (4.16) yields

$$(4.36) \qquad V(c^*(t), p(t))e^{\delta t} + J_t + J_W(dy - c^* + \alpha_p wW) + J_p p\alpha_p$$
$$+ \tfrac{1}{2}J_{WW}(\sigma_p^2 w^{*2} W^2 + \sigma_y^2 + \rho_{py}\sigma_p w^* W\sigma_y) + \tfrac{1}{2}J_{pp}p^2\sigma_p^2$$
$$+ J_{pw}[p\sigma_p w^* W + \rho_{py}\sigma_p\sigma_y p] = 0 .$$

To obtain first-order conditions for a maximum differentiate (4.36) with respect to c and w so that

(4.37) $$V_y(c^*(t),\ p(t))e^{-\delta t} - J_W = 0$$

and

(4.38) $$J_W\alpha_p W + J_{WW}[\sigma_p^2 W^2 w^* + \frac{1}{2}\rho_{py}\sigma_p\sigma_y W] + J_{pW}[p\sigma_p^2 W] = 0\ .$$

Solving (4.38) for w^*

(4.39) $$w^* = -\frac{J_W}{J_{WW}W\sigma_p^2}\alpha_p - \frac{J_{pW}p}{J_{WW}W} - \frac{1}{2}\rho_{py}\frac{\sigma_y}{\sigma_p}\ .$$ [10]

Conditions (4.36) through (4.38) along with the terminal condition

(4.40) $$J[W(T),\ p(T)] = B[W(T),\ p(T)]$$

define optimal values of $c(t)$ and $w(t)$ in terms of $W(t)$ and $p(t)$ for $t \in [0,t]$. Referring again to the Cobb-Douglas iso-elastic marginal utility case set

(4.41) $$V[c(t),\ p(t)] = \frac{1}{\gamma}c(t)^{\gamma}p(t)^{-\beta\gamma}e^{-\delta t}$$

and

(4.42) $$B[W(T),\ p(T)] = \frac{\mu}{\gamma}W(T)^{\gamma}p(T)^{-\beta\gamma}$$

for $(\gamma < 1\ ,\ 1 > \beta > 0)$. Again assume $\alpha_y = \sigma_y = 0$. As before, evaluation of (4.37) yields

(4.43) $$c^*(t) = [J_W(t)p(t)^{\gamma\beta}e^{\delta t}]^{1/1-\gamma}\ .$$

Substituting (4.39) and (4.43) into (4.36) gives

---

[10] Fischer [1975] obtains a similar expression.

$$(4.44)\qquad \left(\frac{1-\gamma}{\gamma}\right)(J_W p^{\beta} e^{\delta t})^{\gamma/\gamma-1} + J_t + \frac{J_W}{J_{WW}}\alpha_p\left(-\frac{J_W\alpha_p}{\sigma_p^2} - J_{pW}p\right) + J_p p\alpha_p$$

$$+ \frac{1}{2}\left(\frac{\sigma_p^2}{J_{WW}}\right)\left(\frac{J_W\alpha_p}{\sigma_p^2} + J_{pW}p\right)^2 + \frac{1}{2}J_{pp}p^2\sigma_p^2 - \frac{J_{pW}}{J_{WW}}p\,(J_W + J_{pW}p\sigma_p^2) .$$

Again consider a trial solution of the form

$$(4.45)\qquad J[W(t), p(t)] = \frac{b(t)}{\gamma}e^{-\delta t}W(t)^{\gamma}p(t)^{-\beta\gamma} .$$

Substituting (4.44) into (4.43) indicates that $b(t)$ must, as in Section 1, satisfy a differential equation of the form

$$(4.46)\qquad \dot{b}(t) = v'b(t) + (1-\gamma)b(t)^{\gamma/\gamma-1} .$$

Here, however

$$(4.47)\qquad v' = \delta + \frac{\gamma}{1-\gamma}\left(\beta - \frac{\alpha_p}{2\sigma_p^2}\right)\alpha_p - [\beta\gamma/2(1-\gamma)][1+\gamma(\beta-1)]\sigma_p^2$$

where $b(t)$ is subject to the boundary condition

$$b(T) = \mu .$$

The solution is of the form of (4.31), i.e.

$$(4.48)\qquad b(t) = \{\epsilon'(1 - e^{\epsilon'(t-T)}) + \mu^{1/1-\gamma}e^{\epsilon'(t-T)}\}^{1-\gamma}$$

where $\epsilon' = v'/(1-\gamma)$. Again $b(t) \geq 0$ for all ϵ' and v' .

To obtain an explicit expression for w^* , the share of wealth held in the asset tied to commodity 2, substitute the appropriate derivatives of (4.44) into (4.39)

$$(4.49) \qquad w^* = \frac{1}{1-\gamma}[(\alpha_p/\sigma_p^2) - \beta\gamma] \ .$$

For $\alpha_p \leq 0$ and $\gamma > 0$, $w^* < 0$: the consumer will sell the second asset short. For $\gamma = 0$ and $\alpha_p = 0$, $w^* = 0$. As $\gamma \to -\infty$ $\lim w^* = \beta$ independent of α_p and σ_p^2.

If commodity 2 is not consumed at all $\beta = 0$ and expression (4.49) becomes

$$(4.49) \qquad \frac{\alpha_p}{(1-\gamma)\sigma_p^2}$$

which has the same sign as α_p. If no price increase is anticipated asset 2 is not held. When commodity 2 is consumed $\beta > 0$ and holdings of asset 2 will be greater if $\gamma < 0$ and actually smaller if $\gamma > 0$. The less risk averse will hold less of asset 2 to reduce expenditure on commodity 2 when its price is high.

Substituting the appropriate derivative of the solution (4.45) into the condition for optimal consumption, expression (4.43), gives

$$(4.50) \qquad c^*(t) = b(t)W(t) \ .$$

By either assuming that $\mu = 0$ or considering a point at which T-t is large the boundary condition will not influence significantly the relationship between optimal consumption and price behavior. In this case $b(t)$ will depend positively on ν'.

Comparing ν' with ν obtained in expression (4.29) for the one-asset case one observes that:

1. For a given level of wealth an increase in the expected rate of price increase α_p increases optimal consumption in the one-asset case if $\gamma > 0$ and lowers it if $\gamma < 0$. In the two-asset case this is true if and only if $\beta > \alpha_p/2\sigma_p^2$. If the opposite is true opportunities for speculation lead the less risk averse to consume less when the rate of price increase rises.

2. If $\alpha_p = \rho_{pr} = 0$ the difference between ν and ν' depends on a term with the sign of γ. Those with degree of relative risk aversion less than one will consume less, for a given level of wealth, in the two-asset case than in the one-asset case while those more risk averse will consume more.

3. An increase in the variance of price movements decreases optimal consumption at a given level of wealth for those with degree of relative risk aversion less than unity, as in the one-asset case. For those with degree of relative risk aversion greater than one increased variance always increases optimal consumption in the two-asset case even if $\gamma < -1/\beta$.

The determinants of the effect of increased relative price uncertainty on optimal savings are, for preferences described by Cobb-Douglas utility functions, the same in the two-period and continuous-time cases. This result suggests that the two-period analysis provides a better insight into situations of permanent increases in uncertainty than into situations of increased uncertainty lasting only briefly.

V. Conclusions

This essay has considered the effect of changes of different types in the distribution of future relative prices on expected welfare and on consumption demand. The results are relevant to at least two areas of economics: international trade and the theory of the consumption function.

In considering the balance-of-payments adjustment mechanism in an economy with Keynesian unemployment, Laursen and Metzler [1950] state the following:

> We therefore believe there is a strong presumption that, as import prices fall and the real income corresponding to a given money income increases, the amount spent on goods and services out of a given money income will fall. (p. 286)

The results in the present essay suggest that there is no such presumption. In the terms adopted above, one may assume income and the prices of domestic goods to be fixed in money terms and consider imports as commodity two of the analysis. Unless the subjective probability distribution of future import prices changes as the result of the initial import price fall expression (4.7) implies that the Laursen-Metzler result will obtain only if the income elasticity of demand for imports is less than the degree of relative risk aversion. Otherwise consumers may react to a fall in import prices by spending more in domestic money terms in the period in which the lower import prices occur. They will be buying imports when the price is low, and, because they are relatively unaverse to risk, will suffer relatively little from transferring expenditure from other periods to take advantage of the "good buy." If the degree of relative risk aversion is one, imports must be necessities for the Laursen-Metzler result to hold.

The price of tradable goods relative to domestic goods is likely to be more variable under a regime of flexible exchange rates than under fixed rates. The results of this essay suggest under what conditions aggregate demand is likely to be higher. If the utility functions is CES and if the degree of relative risk aversion is constant and greater than one but less than two, aggregate demand will be less under a floating rate regime if mean import prices are unchanged.

Theories of the consumption function usually treat money income as exogenous to the household sector. When the supply of labor is elastic, however, money income depends on the number of hours workers in households choose to work, a choice which will, in general, depend on the real wage, a variable which may be interpreted as the price of leisure for the household. Concavity of the utility function unambiguously implies that a decline in income anticipated in future periods will increase savings. The same does not hold for a decline in the real wage: in general the effect of changes in the anticipated real wage on savings will depend on the degree of relative risk aversion and the elasticity of labor supply.

Leland [1968] has demonstrated that increased uncertainty about future income increases savings when attitudes toward risk are characterized by declining absolute risk aversion. Again, when the elasticity of substitution between consumption expenditure and leisure is greater than zero, the effect of increased real wage uncertainty, as opposed to income uncertainty, on savings is ambiguous.

APPENDIX

RISK AVERSION WITH MANY COMMODITIES

Throughout Essays II and III risk aversion is discussed in terms of the partial derivatives of the indirect utility function, $V(y,p)$, with respect to expenditure, y. The measure of absolute risk aversion, for instance, is given by $-V_{yy}/V_y$ and of relative risk aversion by $-yV_{yy}/V_y$. The von Neumann-Morgenstern axioms are stated in terms of consumption of a single good in amount c where utility is a direct function $u(c)$ of c. The corresponding Arrow-Pratt measures of absolute and relative risk aversion are given by $-u''(c)/u'(c)$ and $-cu''(c)/u'(c)$.

In a multi-commodity word, an individual may be considered risk averse if his direct utility function is strictly concave. That strict concavity of the direct utility function implies that the second derivative of the indirect utility function is negative can be demonstrated for the two commodity case. If utility is a direct function of the amounts consumed of two commodities c_1 and c_2, $u(c_1, c_2)$, strict concavity implies $u_{11} < 0$ and $u_{11}u_{22} - u_{12}^2 > 0$. Maximizing u subject to the budget constraint $c_1 + pc_2 \leq y$ where the price of commodity 1 is numeraire one obtains an indirect utility function $V(y,p)$. Furthermore,

$$V_y = u_1 = \frac{1}{p}u_2$$

and

$$V_{yy} = (u_{11}u_{22} - u_{12}^2)/(u_{22} - 2pu_{12} + p^2 u_{11}) \ .$$

The first expression is positive if u is strictly increasing in its arguments, while strict concavity of u implies that the second expression is negative.

Strict concavity of the direct utility function thus implies, for the two-commodity case at least, that the indirect utility function is concave in expenditure. Jensen's inequality implies then that for any given relative price, $\bar{p}$, the consumer prefers a certain expenditure level $\bar{y}$ to an uncertain expenditure level with expected value $\bar{y}$.

In Figure 2.2 consider three indifference curves AA, BB and CC representing utility levels a, b and c, respectively, such that $\frac{1}{2}a + \frac{1}{2}c = b$. Strict concavity of u implies that, for any price level p, the following relationship holds between the minimum expenditure levels required to maintain each utility level

$$\frac{1}{2}y_a(p) + \frac{1}{2}y_c(p) \geq y_b(p) \ .$$

At different relative prices, however, the second derivative of the indirect utility function with respect to expenditure will in general be different, although always negative.

In the case of homothetic utility the measures of relative risk aversion and absolute risk aversion will be invariant to relative prices. If

$$V(y,p) = m(y)g(p)$$

then

$$-yV_{yy}/V_y = -m''(y)y/m'(y)$$

and

$$-V_{yy}/V_y = -m''(y)/m'(y)$$

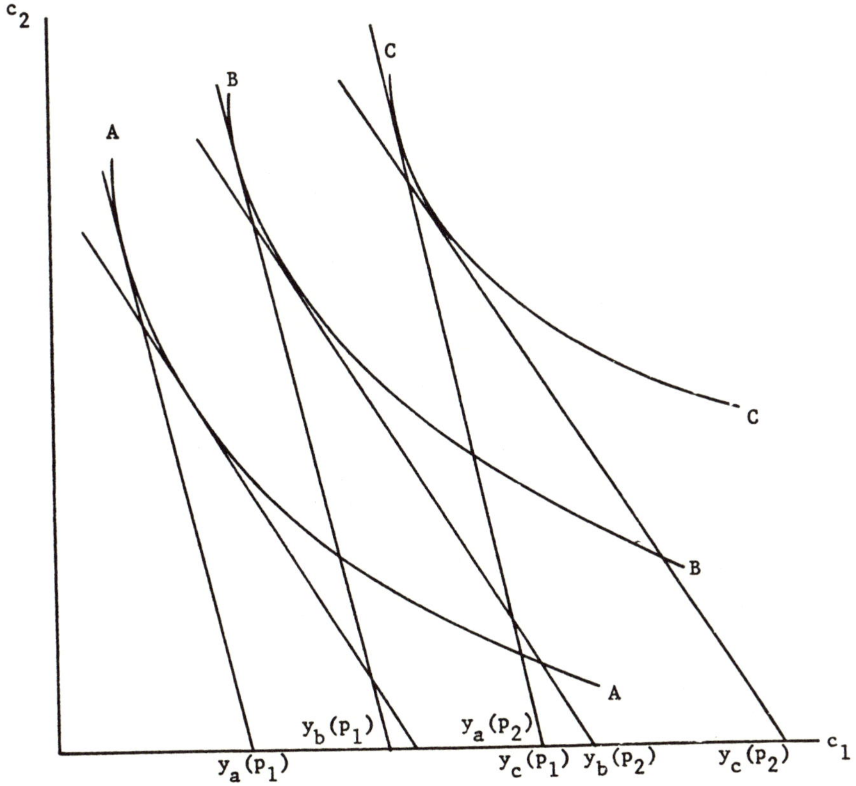

FIGURE 2.2

An additional problem arising in the multi-commodity case is the sensitivity of the derivatives of the indirect utility function with respect to expenditure to the choice of numeraire. From the homogeneity of degree zero of the indirect utility function in prices and expenditure

$$V(y,p,1) = V(\lambda y,\ \lambda p,\ \lambda)\ ,\quad \lambda > 0\ .$$

Defining

$$\hat{V}(\hat{y},\ \hat{p}_1,\ \hat{p}_2)\ ,$$

where $\hat{y} = \lambda y$, $\hat{p}_1 = \lambda p$, $\hat{p}_2 = \lambda$, observe that

$$V_y = \hat{V}_y/\lambda$$

and

$$V_{yy} = \hat{V}_y/\lambda^2\ .$$

The degree of relative risk aversion is, however, invariant to the choice of numeraire since:

$$-\frac{\hat{y}\hat{V}_{yy}}{\hat{V}_y} = -\frac{\lambda_y V_{yy}/\lambda^2}{V_y/\lambda^2} = \frac{-yV_{yy}}{V_y}\ .$$

BIBLIOGRAPHY

Arrow, K. J. [1968]. "The Role of Securities in the Optimal Allocation of Risk-Bearing," Review of Economic Studies, 31, pp. 91-96.

Bawa, V. S. [1975]. "Optimal Rules for Ordering Uncertain Prospects," Journal of Financial Economics, 2, pp. 95-121.

Debreu, G. [1959]. Theory of Value (New Haven: Yale University Press).

Diamond, P. A. and J. E. Stiglitz [1974]. "Increases in Risk and Risk Aversion," Journal of Economic Theory, 8, pp. 337-360.

Epstein, L. [1975]. "A Disaggregate Analysis of Consumer Choice Under Uncertainty," Econometrica, 43, pp. 877-892.

Fischer, S. [1975]. "The Demand for Index Bonds," Journal of Political Economy, 83, pp. 509-534.

Hadar, J. and W. Russell [1969]. "Rules for Ordering Uncertain Prospects," American Economic Review, 59, pp. 25-34.

Hahn, F. [1970]. "Savings under Uncertainty," Review of Economic Studies, 37, pp. 21-24.

Intriligator, M. D. [1971]. Mathematical Optimization and Economic Theory (Englewood Cliffs, N.J.: Prentice Hall).

Kihlstrom, R. E. and L. J. Mirman [1974]. "Risk Aversion with Many Commodities," Journal of Economic Theory, 8, pp. 361-388.

Laursen, S. and L. A. Metzler [1950]. "Flexible Exchange Rates and the Theory of Employment," Review of Economics and Statistics, 32, pp. 281-299.

Leland, H. E. [1968]. "Savings and Uncertainty: The Precautionary Demand for Saving," Quarterly Journal of Economics, 82, pp. 465-473.

Levhari, D. and T. N. Srinivasan [1969]. "Optimal Savings under Uncertainty," Review of Economic Studies, 36, pp. 153-164.

Merton, R. C. [1969]. "Lifetime Portfolio Selection Under Uncertainty: The Continuous-Time Case," Review of Economics and Statistics, 51, pp. 247-257.

__________ [1971]. "Optimum Consumption and Portfolic Rules in a Continuous-Time Model," Journal of Economic Theory, 3, pp. 373-413.

Mirman, L. J. [1971]. "Uncertainty and Optimal Consumption Decisions," Econometrica, 39, pp. 179-185.

Mirrlees, J. A. [1971]. "Optimum Growth and Uncertainty," unpublished paper prepared for I.E.A. Workshop of Economic Theory, Bergen, 1971.

Radner, R. [1968]. "Competitive Equilibrium Under Uncertainty," Econometrica, 36, pp. 31-58.

Rothschild, M. and J. E. Stiglitz [1970]. "Increasing Risk: I. A Definition," Journal of Economic Theory, 2, pp. 225-243.

__________ [1971]. "Increasing Risk: II. Its Economic Consequences," Journal of Economic Theory, 3, pp. 66-84.

Samuelson, P. A. [1972]. "Feasible Price Stability," Quarterly Journal of Economics, 86, pp. 476-493.

Sandmo, A. [1970]. "The Effect of Uncertainty on Saving Decisions," Review of Economic Studies, 37, pp. 353-360.

Sibley, D. S. [1975]. "Permanent and Transitory Income Effects in a Model of Optimal Consumption with Wage Income Uncertainty," Journal of Economic Theory, 11, pp. 68-82.

Stiglitz, J. E. [1969]. "Behavior Towards Risk with Many Commodities," Econometrica, 37, pp. 660-667.

__________ [1972]. "Portfolio Allocation with Many Risky Assets," Mathematical Methods in Investment and Finance. Edited by Szego, G. P. and K. Shell (Amsterdam: North-Holland).

Waugh, F. V. [1944]. "Does the Consumer Benefit from Price Instability," Quarterly Journal of Economics, 58, pp. 602-614.

ESSAY III

SPECIALIZATION, RESERVE LEVELS AND INVESTMENT UNDER UNCERTAINTY IN AN OPEN ECONOMY

I. Uncertainty, Specialization and Optimal Reserve Levels in an Open Economy

Uncertainty in future technology and in future terms of trade will affect welfare and the optimal allocation of resources in an open economy. The effect of uncertainty on the expected welfare of an open economy depends critically on the extent to which economic agents may adjust their consumption, production, savings and portfolio decisions in response to the actual outcome of a random event. In general, as demonstrated in the first essay, increased uncertainty is less likely to reduce expected welfare the greater the *ex post* flexibility of economic agents.

Brainard and Cooper [1968], Batra [1975] and Batra and Russell [1974] have considered the effect of increased price and technological uncertainty on expected welfare and on optimal specialization when production and consumption decisions must precede knowledge of actual price and technological outcomes.

Turnovsky [1974] examines the effect of price and technological uncertainty on welfare and specialization in a one-factor Ricardian model of trade allowing consumption but not production decisions to follow knowledge of outcomes.

All of these studies are one-period analyses which do not consider intertemporal transfer of resources. Nsouli [1975], in a linear production model, and McCabe and Sibley [1975], in a more general context, analyze the effect of export revenue uncertainty on optimal accumulation of capital and reserves. These studies do not consider potential substitutability in production of exports and import substitutes as a factor in deriving demand for reserves, however.

This essay deals with the effect of uncertainty in terms of trade and in technology on expected welfare, optimal production and consumption decisions and on optimal reserve policy. We consider separately two reserve assets, one fixed in value in terms of the import good and the other in terms of the export good. The first could correspond to foreign exchange while the second to inventories of the export good. We allow negative or positive holdings of either reserve. In Part I we assume that no form of wealth is involved in production. Part II examines some implications of introducing productive capital as an asset.

Part I considers the effect of increased uncertainty in terms of trade and in technology on expected welfare, optimal production and consumption and on reserve policy under three regimes. In Section A it is assumed, following Brainard and Cooper [1968], Batra [1975], and Batra and Russell [1974], that no allocation of resources may precede knowledge of outcomes: consumption production, savings and portfolio allocation decisions must be made on the basis of anterior beliefs about relative prices and technology. In Section B consumption is treated as an <u>ex post</u> control while production, savings and portfolio decisions must be made without knowledge of outcomes. Finally Section C allows both production and consumption decisions, but not savings decisions, to occur with knowledge of actual outcomes.

Throughout Part I we assume that the production technology may be represented by the relationship:

$$(0.1) \qquad x_2 = \theta\hat{f}(x_1)\ , \quad \hat{f}' < 0\ , \quad \hat{f}'' \leq 0$$

where x_1 and x_2 represent the domestic production of commodities 1 and 2 respectively. We require nonnegative production:

$$x_1 \geq 0 \ , \quad x_2 \geq 0 \ .$$

The variable θ represents a random term in the production technology with density function $f(\theta)$. We assume

$$(0.2) \qquad \int_{-\infty}^{0} f(\theta)d\theta = 0 \ .$$

$$(0.3) \qquad \int_{0}^{\overline{\theta}} f(\theta)d\theta = 1$$

for some $\overline{\theta} < \infty$ and

$$(0.4) \qquad \int_{0}^{\overline{\theta}} \theta f(\theta)d\theta \equiv E(\theta) = 1 \ .$$

The relative international price of commodity 1 in terms of commodity 2 is given by the random variable p which is unaffected by domestic decisions. We assume, as above, that the density function $g(p)$ has the following properties:

$$(0.5) \qquad \int_{-\infty}^{0} g(p)dp = 0$$

$$(0.6) \qquad \int_{0}^{\overline{p}} g(p)dp = 1$$

for some $\overline{p} < \infty$ and

$$(0.7) \qquad \int_{0}^{\overline{p}} pg(p)dp \equiv E(p) = 1 \ .$$

In considering the effects of price uncertainty we assume

$$(0.8) \qquad F(\theta) = 0 , \quad \theta < 1$$

$$F(\theta) = 1 , \quad \theta \geq 1$$

where

$$F(\theta) \equiv \int_{-\infty}^{\theta} f(x)dx .$$

Similarly, in analyzing technological uncertainty, the assumptions that

$$(0.9) \qquad G(p) = 0 , \quad p < 1$$

$$G(p) = 1 , \quad p \geq 1$$

where

$$G(p) \equiv \int_{-\infty}^{p} g(p)dp$$

are maintained.

It is assumed that aggregate preferences may be represented by the utility function

$$(0.10) \qquad u(c_1, c_2)$$

where c_1 and c_2 represent consumption of commodities 1 and 2 respectively and where u is quasi-concave and increasing in c_1 and c_2. In the two-period analysis the utility function considered is of the form

$$(0.11) \qquad u^1(c_1^1, c_2^1) + u^2(c_1^2, c_2^2)$$

where c_j^i is the consumption of commodity j in period i.

A. Prior Planning of Production and Consumption

We assume that the production and consumption of commodity 1, x_1 and c_1 respectively, are set before the actual value of θ or p is known. Balance of trade equilibrium requires that

$$c_2 = \theta\hat{f}(x_1) + p(x_1 - c_1) \tag{1.1}$$

1. Uncertainty in Terms of Trade

The country chooses x_1 and c_1 to maximize expected utility where

$$\begin{aligned} E[U(c_1, c_2)] &= E[W(c_1, x_1, p)] \\ &\equiv \int_0^{\bar{p}} U[c_1, \hat{f}(x_1) + p(x_1 - c_1)]f(p)dp \end{aligned} \tag{1.2}$$

We demonstrate:

Proposition 1. Increased price uncertainty reduces expected utility when production and consumption decisions precede knowledge of price.

Proof. By Theorem 1 of the first essay increased uncertainty in the distribution of a random variable decreases the expected value of the objective function when it is concave in that variable. Evaluating the second derivative of (1.2) with respect to price yields

$$W_{pp} = (x_1 - c_1)^2 U_{22} \tag{1.3}$$

which is negative if the marginal utility of commodity 2 is diminishing.

The first-order conditions for optimal values of x_1 and c_1 are given by:

$$(1.4) \qquad E[W_x(x_1, c_1, p)] = 0$$

and

$$E[W_c(x_1, c_1, p)] = 0 \ .$$

We may apply Theorem 4 of the first essay to determine the effect of increased uncertainty on optimal production and consumption levels. Increased uncertainty increases or decreases optimal production of commodity 1, x_1^*, as

$$(1.5) \qquad -\bar{W}_{cc}W_{xpp} + \bar{W}_{xc}W_{cpp} \gtrless 0$$

and increases or decreases optimal consumption of commodity 1, c_1^*, as

$$(1.6) \qquad -\bar{W}_{xx}W_{cpp} + \bar{W}_{xc}W_{xpp} \gtrless 0 \ .$$

Evaluating the partial derivatives gives

$$(1.7) \qquad W_{xc} = (U_{12} - pU_{22})[\hat{f}'(x_1) + p]$$

$$W_{cc} = U_{11} - 2pU_{12} + p^2U_{22}$$

$$W_{xx} = \hat{f}''(x)U_2 + U_{22}[\hat{f}'(x) + p]^2$$

$$W_{xpp} = 2(x_1 - c_1)U_{22} + [\hat{f}'(x) + p](x_1 - c_1)^2U_{222}$$

$$W_{cpp} = -2(x_1 - c_1)U_{22} + (x_1 - c_1)^2(U_{122} - U_{222}) \ .$$

Clearly the signs of (1.5) and (1.6) are in general indeterminate. If the initial situation is one of certainty, however, the expected value of a function of the random variable is closely approximated by the function of the expected value and the deviation from the optimality condition under certainty,

$$(1.8) \qquad \hat{f}'(x) + p = 0$$

will be very small.

Assuming an initial situation of certainty we set

$$(1.9) \qquad E(W_{cx}) = 0$$

$$E(W_{cc}) = U_{11} - 2U_{12} + U_{22}$$

$$E(W_{xx}) = -\hat{f}''(x)U_2 \ .$$

Expression (1.5) then has the sign of W_{xpp} . Since the range of variation is small the second term is insignificant. The first term of W_{xpp}

$$(1.10) \qquad 2(x_1 - c_1)U_{22}$$

is negative if $x_1 > c_1$ and positive otherwise. We deduce:

<u>Proposition 2</u>. From an initial situation of certainty introduction of price uncertainty decreases the optimal production of a commodity if it is exported and increases its production if it is imported.

The effect of increased price uncertainty on consumption is given by the sign of

$$(1.11) \qquad W_{cpp} = -2(x_1 - c_1)U_{22} + (x_1 - c_1)^2(U_{122} - U_{222})$$

which is generally indeterminate

Proposition 3. From an initial situation of certainty introduction of price uncertainty increases (decreases) the optimal consumption of commodity 1 if it is exported (imported) and if $U_{122} > U_{222}$ $(U_{122} < U_{222})$.

Under certain restrictions on the third derivatives of the utility functions increased price uncertainty from initial certainty increases (decreases) production of imports (exports) and decreases (increases) consumption of imports (exports) reducing the amount of trade. Specifically, the effect of introducing price uncertainty on the optimal exports of commodity 1, $e_1 = x_1 - c_1$ is, given by the sign of

$$-2[U_{11} - 2U_{12} + U_{22}]e_1U_{22} \tag{1.12}$$

which is always negative for $e_1 > 0$ and positive for $e_1 < 0$.

Proposition 4. When the initial situation is one of certainty increased uncertainty reduces the amount of trade.[1]

2. Uncertainty in Production

Proposition 4 suggests that uncertainty in terms of trade will tend to reduce specialization. In this section we consider the effect of uncertainty in the parameter θ of the production function on optimal production and consumption.

The objective function is now

---

[1]Brainard and Cooper [1968] obtain the result given in Proposition 4 for the case of the quadratic utility function for which $U_{122} = U_{222} = 0$. They do not consider separately the effect of increased uncertainty on production and consumption decisions.

(1.13) $$\int_0^{\bar{\theta}} U(c_1,\ \theta\hat{f}(x_1) + x_1 - c_1) f(\theta) d\theta \equiv E[W(c_1,\ x_1,\ \theta)] \ .$$

We demonstrate:

Proposition 5. Increased output uncertainty reduces expected utility when production and consumption decisions precede the outcome.

Proof. Observe that

(1.14) $$W_{\theta\theta} = U_{22}[\hat{f}(x_1)]^2 < 0$$

and proceed as in the proof of Proposition 1.

The first order conditions for a maximum are

(1.15) $$E[U_1 - U_2] = 0$$

and

(1.16) $$E\{U_2[\theta\hat{f}'(x_1) + 1]\} = 0 \ .$$

The effect of a mean-preserving spread in the distribution of θ on the optimal production and consumption levels is given by the signs of

(1.17) $$-\bar{W}_{cc}W_{x\theta\theta} + \bar{W}_{cx}W_{c\theta\theta}$$

and

(1.18) $$-\bar{W}_{xx}W_{c\theta\theta} + \bar{W}_{cx}W_{x\theta\theta}$$

respectively. Evaluating the partial derivatives gives

$$(1.19) \qquad W_{cx} = (U_{12} - U_{22})[\theta\hat{f}'(x_1) + 1]$$

$$W_{xx} = \theta\hat{f}''(x_1)U_2 + [\theta\hat{f}'(x_1) + 1]^2 U_{22}$$

$$W_{cc} = U_{11} - 2U_{12} + U_{22}$$

$$W_{x\theta\theta} = 2\hat{f}'(x_1)\hat{f}(x_1)U_{22} + [\theta\hat{f}'(x_1) + 1]\hat{f}(x_1)^2 U_{222}$$

$$W_{c\theta\theta} = \hat{f}(x_1)^2(U_{122} - U_{222}) \; .$$

If the initial situation is one of certainty then

$$(1.20) \qquad E(W_{cx}) = 0 \; .$$

Since the first term in the expression for $W_{x\theta\theta}$ is negative we may state:

<u>Proposition 6</u>. From an initial position of certainty increased production uncertainty increases the optimal production of commodity 1, the commodity with certain technology.

From the expression for $W_{c\theta\theta}$ we may conclude:

<u>Proposition 7</u>. When there is initially no uncertainty increased production uncertainty increases or decreases the optimal consumption of commodity 1 as $U_{122} \gtrless U_{222}$.

The effect of introducing production uncertainty is reduced production of the commodity with uncertain technology. The effect on consumption is ambiguous, depending on third derivatives of the utility function. When $U_{122} = U_{222}$ the consumption effect is zero. In this case increased production uncertainty increases trade and specialization if commodity 2 is initially imported and reduces trade and specialization if commodity

2 is initially exported.

In summary, when uncertainty derives from uncertainty in the terms of trade the optimal response is usually trade reduction, with both production and consumption adjusting. When it is caused by increased uncertainty in technology the optimal response is reduced production of the commodity whose technology is uncertain and the direction of the optimal response of consumption is ambiguous.

3. Optimal Reserve Holdings under Uncertainty

The discussion in Sections 1 and 2 assumed that balance of trade equilibrium must be maintained within each period. No intertemporal transfers through international borrowing or lending or accumulation of inventories were introduced. We now modify this assumption to consider the effect of increased price and production uncertainty on optimal reserve policy.

We introduce a reserve with value fixed in terms of commodity 1. We analyze optimal borrowing or lending in a two period model in which debts incurred in the first period are repaid at the end of the second period.

The level of reserve holdings is denoted as s . The availability of commodity 1 for consumption in period 1 is given at c_1^1 and of commodity 2 at c_2^1 . Holdings of asset 1 represent a depletion in period 1 consumption of commodity 1 from the initial availability at c_1^1 .

The problem is to choose s , x_1^2 and c_1^2 to maximize

$$(1.21) \qquad U^1(c_1^1 - s,\ c_2^1) + E[U(c_1^2,\ c_2^2)]$$

subject to the requirement of 0 debt at the end of period 2:

(1.22) $$c_2^2 = \theta\hat{f}(x_1^2) + p(x_1^2 + s - c_1^2) .$$

First-order conditions for a maximum are

(1.23) $$-U_1^1 + E[pU_2^2] = 0$$

$$E[U_2^2(\theta\hat{f}'(x_1^2) + p)] = 0$$

$$E[U_1^2 + pU_2^2] = 0 .$$

The effect of increased price uncertainty on the optimal value of s_1 has the same sign as

(1.24) $$-\frac{1}{\Delta}[\Delta_{11}W_{1pp} + \Delta_{12}W_{2pp} + \Delta_{13}W_{3pp}]$$

where

(1.25) $$W(s, x_1^2, c_1^2, p, \theta) = U^1(c_1^1 - s, c_2) + U^2(c_1^2, c_2^2)$$

and

(1.26) $$\frac{1}{\Delta}\{\Delta_{ij}\} = \{\overline{W}_{ij}\}^{-1} , \quad i, j = 1, 2\ 3 .$$

Differentiating (1.25) gives

$$(1.27) \qquad W_{11} = U_{11}^1 + p^2U_{22}^2$$

$$W_{12} = pU_{22}^2(\theta\hat{f}' + p)$$

$$W_{13} = pU_{21}^2 - p^2U_{22}^2$$

$$W_{22} = U_2^2\theta\hat{f}'' + U_{22}^2(\theta\hat{f}' + p)^2$$

$$W_{23} = (U_{12} - pU_{22}^2)(\theta\hat{f}' + p)$$

$$W_{33} = U_{11}^2 - 2pU_{12}^2 + p^2U_{22}^2$$

$$W_{1pp} = U_{22}^2e_1 + pU_{222}^2e_1^2$$

$$W_{2pp} = U_{22}^2e_1 + (\theta\hat{f}' + p)U_{222}^2e_1^2$$

$$W_{3pp} = -U_{22}^2e_1 + (U_{122}^2 - pU_{222}^2)e_1^2$$

where $e_1 = (x_1^2 + s - c_1^2)$.

Limiting our analysis, as before, to situations of initial certainty expression (1.24) becomes

$$(1.28) \qquad (U_2^2\hat{f}'')[(U_{11}^2 - U_{12}^2)(U_{22}^2e_1 + U_{222}^2e_1^2) - (U_{21}^2 - U_{22}^2)U_{122}^2e_1^2]$$

which is of indeterminate sign. In the case of an additively-separable utility function, however, $U_{12} = U_{122} = 0$ and expression (1.28) has the same sign as

$$(1.29) \qquad U_{22}e_1 + U_{222}e_1^2 \ .$$

If $U_{222} > 0$, i.e., if marginal utility diminishes at a diminishing rate, expression (1.29) is positive if commodity 1 is imported and of ambiguous sign if it is exported. Thus:

Proposition 8. In the case of an additively-separable utility function characterized by a diminishing rate of diminishing marginal utility introduction of price uncertainty increases optimal holdings of the asset with price fixed in terms of commodity 1 if it is imported while the effect is ambiguous if it is exported.

The condition $U_{222} > 0$ implies that the detrimental effect of variation in the consumption of commodity 2 is reduced as the level of its consumption increases. This effect tends to increase optimal reserve holdings. When commodity 1 is imported, increased reserve holdings reduce the variation in commodity 2 consumption and increase expected utility. In this case price uncertainty unambiguously increases optimal reserve holdings. If, however, commodity 1 is exported increased reserve holdings increase uncertainty in consumption of commodity 2 in period 2 by increasing the amount of commodity 1 exported.

To consider the effect of introducing technological uncertainty on optimal reserve holding we obtain the expressions

(1.30) $$W_{1\theta\theta} = pU_{222}^2 \hat{f}(x)^2$$

$$W_{2\theta\theta} = pU_{22}^2 \hat{f}'\hat{f}(x)$$

$$W_{3\theta\theta} = (U_{122}^2 + pU_{222}^2)\hat{f}(x)^2 \; .$$

Substituting (1.27) and (1.30) into the expression for the effect of increased technological uncertainty on optimal reserve holdings gives

(1.31) $$U_2^2 \hat{f}''\hat{f}(x)^2 [(U_{11}^2 - U_{12}^2)U_{222}^2] - (U_{21}^2 - U_{22}^2)U_{122}^2 \; .$$

which is generally ambiguous in sign. If, however, $U_{12} = U_{122} = 0$ and $U_{222} > 0$ it is positive.

Proposition 9. In the case of an additively-separable utility function characterized by a diminishing rate of diminishing marginal utility introduction of technological uncertainty increases optimal reserve holdings.

B. Consumption as an Ex Post Control

We now turn to the case in which the production decision must precede knowledge of the outcome of the random event while the consumption decision may follow it. Consumers maximize

(2.1) $$U(c_1, c_2)$$

subject to the constraint that the value of consumption equal y, the value of production at international prices. This implies

(2.2) $$pc_1 + c_2 = px_1 + \theta\hat{f}(x_1) \equiv y .$$

First-order conditions for a maximum are:

(2.3) $$U_1(c_1, c_2) = p$$

and

$$U_2(c_1, c_2) = 1 .$$

Expressions (2.2) and (2.3) implicitly define functions $c_1(p, Y)$ and $c_2(p, Y)$ which, upon substitution into (2.1), yield the indirect utility function

(2.4) $$V(y,p) = U[c_1(y,p), c_2(y,p)] .$$

The country chooses a level of output of commodity 1, x_1^*, to maximize the expected value of the indirect utility function:

(2.5) $$E[V(px_1 + \theta\hat{f}(x_1), p)] \equiv E[W(x_1, p, \theta)] .$$

In Sections 1 and 2 below we consider the effects of increased uncertainty in international prices and technology on welfare and on the optimal production of commodity 1.

1. Uncertainty in Terms of Trade

By Theorem 1 of the first essay an increase in price uncertainty will reduce expected utility if $W(x_1, p, \theta)$ is a concave function of p and increase expected utility if it is a convex function of p. Differentiating W twice with respect to p yields

$$(2.6) \qquad W_{pp} = x_1^2 V_{yy} + 2x_1 V_{yp} + V_{pp} \text{ .}$$[2]

On the basis of the Slutsky relationship

$$(2.7) \qquad V_p = -cV_y$$

one can derive the relationships

$$(2.8) \qquad V_{yp} = -cV_{yy} - \frac{\partial c}{\partial y} V_y$$

and

$$(2.9) \qquad V_{pp} = c\left(\frac{\partial c}{\partial y} - \frac{\partial c}{\partial p}\right)V_y + c^2 V_{yy}$$

so that expression (2.6) is equivalent to:

$$(2.10) \qquad W_{pp} = -\left[2(x_1 - c_1)\frac{\partial c_1}{\partial y} + \left(\frac{\partial c_1}{\partial p}\right)_c\right]V_y + (x_1 - c_1)^2 V_{yy} \text{ .}$$

---

[2] Turnovsky [1974] also obtains this expression.

where

$$(2.11) \qquad \left(\frac{\partial y}{\partial p}\right)_c = \frac{\partial c_1}{\partial p} - c\,\frac{\partial c}{\partial y}$$

the income-compensated price elasticity.

The second term is negative whenever the marginal utility of income is diminishing. The sign of the first term is indeterminate. If commodity 1 is imported and non-inferior it is positive, however. From (2.12) we derive the following propositions:

Proposition 11. If $\partial c_1/\partial y > 0$ increased price uncertainty is more likely to raise expected utility when commodity 1 is imported than when it is exported.

When commodity 1 is imported a positive income effect of a high relative price of commodity 1 will lower the demand for commodity 1 when its price is high while if it is exported a positive income effect raises the demand for commodity 1 when its price is high.[3]

Proposition 12. A positive effect of increased price uncertainty on expected utility is more likely the higher the income-compensated price elasticity of demand for commodity 1.

---

[3]From (2.8)

$$\frac{\partial c_1}{\partial y} = -\frac{V_{yp}}{V_y} - \left(\frac{c_1}{y}\right)\frac{V_{yy}y}{V_y}$$

and is likely to be positive if c_1/y and the degree of relative risk aversion are large. Since $y = pc_1 + c_2$

$$\frac{\partial c_2}{\partial y} = 1 + \frac{pV_{yp}}{V_y} + \left(\frac{pc_1}{y}\right)\frac{V_{yy}y}{V_y}$$

It is important to note that the sign of the income effect is sensitive to the choice of numeraire.

A high price elasticity of demand implies that the elasticity of substitution in consumption between commodities 1 and 2 is great. When the commodities are close substitutes transferring expenditure between commodities affects utility to a lesser degree than otherwise.

Finally from the second term of expression (2.11) we derive:

Proposition 13. Increased price uncertainty is more likely to lower expected utility when the volume of trade is high and consumers are risk averse.

A greater volume of trade implies greater variation in income due to variation in the terms of trade.

When consumption is only an *ex ante* control, the case analyzed in Section A,

$$(2.12) \qquad \frac{\partial x}{\partial p} = \frac{\partial x}{\partial y} = 0$$

in which case expression (2.12) reduces to

$$(2.13) \qquad (x_1 - c_1)^2 V_{yy}$$

which is always negative.

A first-order condition for an optimal value of x_1, the production of commodity 1, is

$$(2.14) \qquad E[W_x] = E\{[p + \hat{f}'(x_1)]V_y\} = 0 \ .$$

The effect on the optimal value of x_1 of increased price uncertainty has the same sign as

$$(2.15) \qquad W_{xpp} = -2\,\frac{\partial c}{\partial y}\,V_y - \left[2(x_1 - c_1)\frac{\partial c_1}{\partial y} + \left(\frac{\partial c_1}{\partial p}\right)_c\right][p + \hat{f}'(x_1)]V_{yy}$$
$$+ 2(x_1 - c_1)V_{yy} + (x_1 - c_1)^2[p + \hat{f}'(x_1)]V_{yyy} \; .$$

If the initial situation is one of certainty the condition

$$(2.16) \qquad p + \hat{f}'(x_1) = 0$$

will be met. Expression (2.15) then becomes

$$(2.17) \qquad W_{xpp} = 2\left[-\frac{\partial c_1}{\partial y}\,V_y + (x_1 - c_1)V_{yy}\right] .$$

With some manipulation expression (2.17) may be shown to have the same sign as

$$(2.18) \qquad -Z_y + \left(\frac{c_1 - x_1}{c_1}\right)R$$

where

$$Z_y \equiv \frac{dc_1}{dy}\,\frac{y}{c_1} \, ,$$

the income elasticity of demand for commodity 1 and

$$R \equiv \frac{-V_{yy}y}{V_y}$$

the degree of relative risk aversion. We deduce:

Proposition 14. From an initial position of certainty introducing price uncertainty reduces the optimal production of commodity 1 when the share of imports times the degree of relative risk aversion is less than the income elasticity of demand for commodity 1. If it is greater the optimal production of commodity 1 is increased by increased price uncertainty.

A high degree of risk-aversion leads to an increase in commodity 1 production when commodity 1 is imported and a decrease when it is exported. In either case, however, a high income elasticity of demand for commodity 1 creates an incentive to reduce production to reduce the positive correlation of income and price. Hence, even when commodity 1 is imported increased price uncertainty may _lower_ production of commodity 1, increasing specialization.

2. Uncertainty in Production

We now consider the effects of mean-preserving spreads in the distribution of the production parameter θ when $p = 1$ with certainty. The effect of increased technological uncertainty on expected utility is given by the sign of

$$W_{\theta\theta} = \hat{f}(x_1)^2 V_{yy} \tag{2.19}$$

which is negative for all risk-averse individuals. The ability to choose consumption _ex post_ does not introduce the possibility that increased _technological_ uncertainty will increase expected utility.

The effect of increased uncertainty on the optimal production of commodity 1 is given by the sign of

$$W_{x\theta\theta} = \hat{f}'(x_1)V_{yy} + \hat{f}(x_1)^2[\hat{f}'(x_1) + p]V_{yyy} . \tag{2.20}$$

Assuming, as before, an initial situation of certainty, then

$$(2.21) \qquad \hat{f}'(x_1) + p = 0$$

and expression (2.20) reduces to

$$(2.22) \qquad W_{x\theta\theta} = \hat{f}'(x_1)V_{yy}$$

which is positive for risk-averse individuals. Combining this result with Propositions 5 and 6 above we state:

Proposition 15. Introducing production uncertainty reduces expected welfare and increases output of the commodity not subject to technological uncertainty, when production is an *ex ante* control.

This result is independent of the economy's ability to adjust consumption *ex post*. Technological uncertainty in a small open economy, unlike price uncertainty, affects utility only through its effect on income.

3. Optimal Reserve Holdings under Uncertainty

We now consider the effect of uncertainty on optimal reserve holdings. The price of the asset is the same as that of commodity 1. The optimizing small country chooses reserve holdings in amount s and period 2 production of commodity 1, x, to maximize

$$(2.23) \qquad V^1(y^1 - s) + E\{V^2[\theta\hat{f}(x) + p(x+s), p]\} \equiv E[W(s, x, p, \theta)]$$

where y^1 is given period 1 consumption.

First-order conditions for a maximum are given by:

$$(2.24) \qquad -V_y^1 + E[pV_y^2] = 0$$

$$E\{V_y^2[\theta\hat{f}'(x) + p]\} = 0 \ .$$

The effect of increased price uncertainty on the optimal value of s is given by the sign of the expression

$$(2.25) \qquad -\bar{W}_{xx}W_{spp} + \bar{W}_{sx}W_{xpp} \ .$$

If the initial situation is one of certainty the second term is zero. The first term has the same sign as W_{spp} . In general the sign of this term is very difficult to determine. If, however, commodity 1 is not consumed the effect of increased uncertainty is given by the sign of the expression:

$$(2.26) \qquad 2V_{yy}^2(x+s) + pV_{yyy}^2(x+s)^2 \ .$$

Decreasing absolute risk aversion implies the first term is negative and the second positive. In the case of constant relative risk aversion expression (2.26) has the same sign as

$$(2.26') \qquad \left[\frac{p(x+s)}{y}(1+R) - 2\right]$$

where

$$(2.27) \qquad R \equiv -yV_{yy}/V_y$$

the Arrow-Pratt measure of relative risk aversion. Expression (2.26) is likely to be negative either when the share of export revenue, in total income, $p(x+s)/y$ is small or when R , the degree of relative risk aversion is small. We state:

Proposition 16. If exports are not domestically consumed the introduction of export price uncertainty is likely to reduce optimal inventories of export commodities when the share of exports in total revenue or the degree of risk aversion is small. Otherwise optimal domestic asset holdings are likely to increase.

When the degree of relative risk aversion is less than or equal to unity expression (2.26) is unambiguously negative when exports account for less than all of period 2 expenditure; when $(x+s)/y \leq 1$ relative risk aversion less than unity is sufficient for increased price uncertainty to lower optimal export inventories.

If the asset is denominated in terms of commodity 2, the imported commodity, the objective function becomes:

$$(2.23') \qquad V^1(y^1 - s) + E[V^2(\theta\hat{f}(x) + s + px,\ p)] .$$

Again assuming that the export commodity is not consumed domestically the effect of increased price uncertainty on optimal foreign exchange holdings is

$$(2.26') \qquad V^2_{yyy}(x+s)^2$$

which is always positive for preferences characterized by decreasing absolute risk aversion. Increasing foreign exchange holdings does not increase uncertainty in period 2 income, unlike increasing inventories of exports.

Proposition 17. If exports are not consumed domestically introducing export price uncertainty increases optimal holdings of foreign reserves.

The effect of introducing technological uncertainty on optimal reserve holdings of either kind is of the same sign as

$$W_{s\theta\theta} = V_{yyy}^2 f(x_1)^2$$

which is, again, always positive when absolute risk aversion is decreasing.

When uncertainty is due to technology rather than price variation, increased reserve holdings do not contribute to income uncertainty. Hence, when $V_{yyy} > 0$, increased uncertainty increases optimal savings. Combining this result with Proposition 9 of Section A we may state:

Proposition 18. When (1) marginal utility diminishes at a diminishing rate and (2) production is an *ex ante* control increased technological uncertainty increases optimal reserve holdings.

C. Production and Consumption as *ex post* Controls

We now assume that x_1, the production of commodity 1, as well as c_1, commodity 1 consumption, may be determined after knowledge of the price or technological outcome is available. We consider the effects of price and technological uncertainty on expected utility and on optimal savings decision.

The country chooses c_1 and x_1 to maximize

(3.1) $$U(c_1, c_2)$$

subject to the constraint that the value of consumption equal the value of production at international prices. This implies, as before, that

(3.2) $$pc_1 + c_2 = px_1 + \hat{\theta f}(x_1) \equiv y \ .$$

Substituting (3.2) into (3.1) and differentiating with respect to c_1 and x_1 yields the following first-order conditions for a maximum

(3.3) $$U_1(c_1, c_2) = p$$

$$U_2[\hat{\theta f}'(x_1) + p] = 0 \ .$$

The second equation of (3.3) is also a condition for maximizing y subject to price and the production possibility locus. The problem may then be decomposed into two parts: (1) selecting x_1 to maximize y, (2) selecting c_1 to maximize (3.1) subject to

(3.4) $$pc_1 + c_2 = y \ .$$

Section B derived the demand functions $c_1(y,p)$ and $c_2(y,p)$ and the corresponding indirect utility function $V(y,p)$ from the second part of this procedure. The first part may then be represented as choosing x_1 to maximize

$$V(y,p) \tag{3.5}$$

The first-order condition for a maximum is

$$\theta\hat{f}'(x_1) + p = 0 . \tag{3.6}$$

1. Uncertainty in Terms of Trade

We assume the technological parameter is fixed at 1. To consider the effects of a mean-preserving spread in the distribution of p on expected utility we determine whether utility is a concave or convex function of price. Differentiating (3.5) twice with respect to p yields

$$\left[\frac{dx_1}{dp} - \left(\frac{dc_1}{dp}\right)_{\bar{c}} - 2(x_1 - c_1)\frac{dc}{dy}\right]V_y + (x_1 - c_1)^2 V_{yy} \tag{3.7}$$

Differentiating (3.6) yields

$$\frac{dx_1}{dp} = -[\hat{f}''(x_1)]^{-1} . \tag{3.8}$$

The first term of expression (3.7) is positive if commodity 1 is imported and non-inferior or exported and inferior. The second term is negative for all risk-averse individuals. From expression (3.7) we derive:

Proposition 19. An increase in price uncertainty is more likely to increase expected utility (1) the larger the price elasticity of supply of commodity 1, (2) the larger the price elasticity of demand for commodity 1, (3) the larger (smaller) the income elasticity of demand for commodity 1 if it is non-inferior and imported (exported) and (4) the smaller the amount of trade and the degree of risk aversion.

In general increased price uncertainty is more likely to increase welfare when opportunities for substitution in production and consumption are large and the exposure to risk and the degree of risk aversion are small.

2. Uncertainty in Production

We now assume that the price is fixed at 1 and consider the effect on expected utility of a mean-preserving spread in the prior probability distribution of the production parameter θ . To determine whether utility is a concave or convex function of θ we differentiate the indirect utility function (3.5) twice with respect to θ to obtain

$$(3.9) \qquad \hat{f}'(x_1)\frac{dx_1}{d\theta}V_y + \hat{f}(x_1)^2 V_{yy} \; .$$

Differentiating (3.6) yields

$$(3.10) \qquad \frac{dx_1}{d\theta} = -\frac{\hat{f}'(x_1)}{\theta\hat{f}''(x_1)} \; .$$

Expression (3.9) may now be written as

$$(3.11) \qquad \frac{-[\hat{f}'(x_1)]^2}{\theta\hat{f}''(x_1)}V_y + \hat{f}(x_1)^2 V_{yy}$$

which has the same sign, at $\theta = 1$, as

$$\sigma - \frac{\hat{f}(x_1)}{y} R$$

where

$$\sigma = \frac{-\hat{f}_1'(x)^2}{\hat{f}''(x_1)\hat{f}(x_1)}$$

the elasticity of substitution in production. We deduce

Proposition 20. When the production decision follows knowledge of technological outcomes increased uncertainty will increase expected utility when the elasticity of substitution in production exceeds the product of the share of production of the commodity with uncertain technology in income and the degree of relative risk aversion. If this condition is reversed increased technological uncertainty reduces expected utility.

In the case of the logarithmic utility function $(R = 1)$, the elasticity of substitution need only exceed the share of commodity 2 production in income for increased uncertainty to raise expected utility.

Propositions 19 and 20 suggest two properties about the optimal choice of technology under uncertainty. First, in the presence of uncertainty in the terms of trade, a technology less productive in the sense of yielding less output of commodity 2 for a given output of commodity 1 at the point where the marginal rate of substitution equals the expected price may nevertheless yield higher expected utility or income because it is characterized by a greater elasticity of substitution in production.[4]

This result is illustrated by a second-order Taylor series expansion of expected income about the expected price $\bar{p}$

---

[4] This observation has been made by Berry and Hymer [1969].

$$(3.12) \qquad E(y) = [\hat{f}(x_1^*) + \bar{p}x_1^*] - [1/\hat{f}''(x_1^*)]\sigma_p^2$$

where $\sigma_p^2 = E[(p-\bar{p})^2]$ and where x_1^* is defined by

$$-\hat{f}'(x_1^*) = \bar{p} .$$

Now consider an alternative technique $\hat{g}(x_1)$ such that $\hat{g}(x_1^*) > \hat{f}(x_1^*)$, $\hat{g}'(x_1^*) = \hat{f}'(x_1^*) = p$, and $\hat{g}''(x_1^*) < \hat{f}''(x_1^*)$. Technique f will yield higher expected income if

$$(3.13) \qquad \hat{g}(x_1^*) - \hat{f}(x_1^*) < 1/(\hat{g}''(x_1^*)) - 1/(\hat{f}''(x_1^*)) .$$

Second, a particular technology more uncertain than another in the sense of yielding a riskier output of commodity 2 for a given output of commodity 1 may yield a higher level of expected utility or income even though its expected production of commodity two for a given output of commodity 1 is smaller for all values of x_1. Expected income in terms of a Taylor-series approximation around $E(\theta) = 1$ is

$$(3.14) \qquad E(y) = x_1^* + \hat{f}(x_1^*) - (1/\hat{f}'')\sigma_\theta^2$$

where

$$1 + \hat{f}'(x_1^*) = 0 \quad \text{and} \quad \sigma_\theta^2 = E(\theta-1)^2 .$$

We introduce an alternative technology $\psi\hat{f}(x)$ where $E(\psi) > E(\theta)$ and $\sigma_\psi^2 < \sigma_\theta^2$. The second technology yields a higher expected income only if

$$(3.15) \qquad x_1^{**} + \overline{\psi}\hat{f}(x_1^{**}) - x_1^* - \hat{f}(x_1^*) > (1/\overline{\psi}\hat{g}'')\sigma_\psi^2 - (1/\hat{f}'')\sigma_\theta^2$$

where $\bar{\psi} = E(\psi)$ and $1 + \overline{\psi}\hat{f}'(x_1^{**}) = 0$.

This result is illustrated in Figure 2.1. A non-random technology

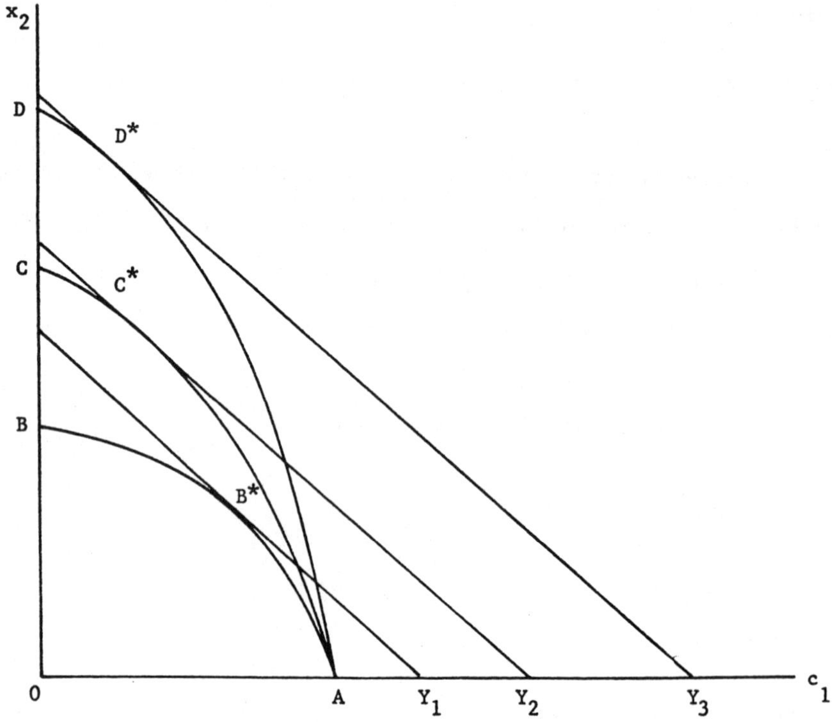

FIGURE 2.1

is represented by the transformation surface AC . A random technology results in the transformation surface AB with probability 1/2 and AD with probability 1/2 . For any value of x_1 the expected value of x_2 is greater under the nonrandom technology.

Income with the non-random technology is Y_2 . With random technology it is Y_1 with probability 1/2 and Y_3 with probability 1/2 where $\frac{1}{2}Y_1 + \frac{1}{2}Y_3 > Y_2$.

3. Optimal Reserve Holdings under Uncertainty

We now allow transfer of resources between two periods by saving or borrowing. As before we alternatively consider two types of assets: first, one with value fixed in terms of the exported commodity and, secondly, one fixed in terms of the imported commodity.

When the reserve asset is, for instance, inventories of the exported commodity an optimizing society will choose s to maximize

$$V^1(y^1 - s) + E[V^2(y^2 + ps,\ p)] \equiv E[W(s,p)] \tag{3.16}$$

where

$$y^2 \equiv \hat{f}(x_1) + px_1 \tag{3.17}$$

and y^1 is given income in period 1. The first-order condition for a maximum is

$$-V_y^1 + E[pV_y^2] = E[W_s] . \tag{3.18}$$

The effect of increased price uncertainty is given by the sign of W_{spp} which, again, is difficult to analyze in the general case. If the exported commodity is not consumed domestically, however, it is

$$\left[2(x+s) + p\frac{\partial x}{\partial p}\right]V_{yy}^2 + pV_{yyy}^2 \ . \tag{3.19}$$

Risk aversion implies the first term is negative while decreasing absolute risk aversion would indicate a positive sign on the second term.

Comparing expression (3.19) above for the case in which production is an <u>ex post</u> control to expression (2.26) in Part B for the case in which the production decision occurs before the fact one observes that they are the same with the addition, in the <u>ex post</u> case, of the presumably negative term, $p\frac{\partial x}{\partial p}V_{yy}$. We deduce

<u>Proposition 21</u>. Increased price uncertainty is more likely to reduce optimal reserve holdings when the production decision is made <u>ex post</u> than when it is made <u>ex ante</u>.

The increased flexibility in the first case reduces the exposure of income to increased price variation. Thus increased price variation leads to less income variation to generate a demand for savings.

In the case of constant relative risk aversion expression (3.19) has the same sign as

$$-Z_p + \left[\frac{p(x+s)}{y}(1+R) - 2\right] \tag{3.20}$$

where

$$Z_p = \frac{\partial x}{\partial p}\frac{p}{x+s}$$

the price elasticity of export supply and

$$R = -yV_{yy}/V_y \ .$$

Expression (3.20) is lower than the comparable condition for the case in which production is an ex ante control by the value Z_p . Even when $R > 1$ and the share of export revenue in income is near 1 increased price uncertainty will lower optimal savings when the responsiveness of production to price variation is great.

When the reserve asset is fixed in terms of the commodity 2, the imported commodity under our simplifying assumption, the maximand is

$$(3.16') \qquad V^1(y^1 - s) + E[V^2(y^2 + s,\ p)] = E[W(s,p)]$$

where, again

$$(3.17) \qquad y^2 \equiv \hat{f}(x_1) + px_1 \ .$$

If the exported commodity is not consumed domestically the effect of increased export price uncertainty on optimal foreign reserve holdings has the sign of

$$(3.19') \qquad \frac{\partial x}{\partial p}V^2_{yy} + x^2 V^2_{yyy}$$

which, unlike the comparable condition for the case in which production is an ex ante control (expression (2.26')); is not necessarily positive. In the case of constant relative risk aversion condition (3.19') has the same sign as

$$(3.20') \qquad -Z_p + \frac{px}{y}(1+R) \ .$$

If, say, $R = 1$ and $Z_p = 1$ export revenue would have to produce fifty percent of income for increased export price uncertainty to raise optimal foreign reserve holdings.

The effect of technological uncertainty on optimal reserve holdings is given by the sign of

$$(3.21) \qquad W_{s\theta\theta} = -V_{yy}[(f')^2/\theta\hat{f}''] + V^2_{yyy}(\hat{f})^2$$

where

$$(3.22) \qquad W(s,\theta) \equiv V^2(y^1 - s) + V^2[\theta\hat{f}(x_1) + s + x] \ .$$

The first term of expression (3.21) is negative and the second positive. At $\theta = 1$ it has the same sign as

$$-\sigma + [\hat{f}(x_1)/y](1+R)$$

where

$$\sigma = -(\hat{f}')^2/\hat{f}\cdot\hat{f}''$$

the elasticity of substitution in production.

<u>Proposition 22</u>. The effect of increased technological uncertainty on optimal savings when production is an <u>ex post</u> control is generally ambiguous. It is negative when the elasticity of substitution exceeds the product of the share of commodity 2 production in income and one plus the degree of relative risk aversion.

If $\sigma = 1$ and $R = 1$ commodity 2 production must constitute at least fifty percent of total production for increased technological uncertainty to increase optimal savings.

II. Investment and Specialization under Uncertainty in an Open Economy

Part I considered the effect of increased uncertainty on expected welfare and on optimal production, consumption and reserve levels in a two-sector economy in which savings does not contribute to the productive capacity of the economy. This part introduces productive capital explicitly as a store of value. It is assumed throughout that the sectoral allocation of capital must antecede knowledge of uncertain outcomes while labor allocation and consumption decisions may occur once outcomes are known. Only uncertainty in the terms of trade is treated.

Section A considers the effect of increased relative price uncertainty on expected utility under these assumptions. Section B derives the effect of increased price uncertainty on optimal investment and reserve holdings for a particular class of production functions. Finally, Section C considers the effect of price uncertainty on specialization patterns in a multi-factor context.

A. Expected Utility and Relative Price Uncertainty

The objective of the economy is the maximization of expected utility over two periods. In terms of the indirect utility functions V^1 and V^2 the objective function is

$$(4.1) \qquad E[V^1(y^1, p^1) + V^2(y^2, p^2)]$$

where y^i represents consumption expenditures in period i in terms of the price of commodity 2 while p^i represents the relative price of commodity 1 in period i. The price p^1 is known and set at unity; p^2, henceforth denoted p, is a random variable with probability density function $f(p)$ of compact support.

Consumption expenditure in period 1 is period 1 income q^1, less investment in capital, K, and in reserves, S:

$$(4.2) \qquad y^1 = q^1 - K - S .$$

Period 2 consumption expenditure is the value of period 2 output q^2 given by the technological relationship

$$(4.3) \qquad q^2 = pF^1(K_1, L_1) + F^2(K_2, L_2)$$

plus the value of reserves, S subject to

$$(4.4) \qquad K_1 + K_2 \leq K , \quad L_1 + L_2 \leq L ,$$

where L is the given aggregate labor supply. The production function F^1 and F^2 are linear homogeneous and twice differentiable.

Values of K_1, K_2, and S, the <u>ex ante</u> controls, must be selected before p is known; L_1 and L_2 may be selected subsequently.

For given values of the ex ante control variables a first-order condition for an optimal allocation of labor is given by

$$(4.5)\qquad [pF_L^1(K_1, L_1) - F_L^2(K_1, L - L_1)] \begin{cases} = 0\ ; & 0 < L_1 < L \\ > 0\ ; & L_1 = L \\ < 0\ ; & L_1 = 0 \end{cases}$$

which states simply that the value of the marginal product of labor in each sector must be equal if labor is employed at positive levels in both sectors. Expression (4.5) implicitly defines an optimal value L_1 as a function of K_1 , K_2 and p . We denote this as

$$(4.6)\qquad L_1^* = L(K_1, K_2, p)\ .$$

Substituting (4.6) into expression (4.3) provides an expression for the value of output in terms of the ex ante control variables K_1 and K_2 and p ,

$$(4.8)\qquad E[W(K_1, K_2, p)] = V^1(q^1 - K_1 - K_2 - S_1) + E\{V^2[R(K_1, K_2, p) + S, p]\}\ .$$

Whether or not increased price uncertainty increases or decreases expected welfare depends on whether W is a convex or concave function of p . Differentiating (4.8):

$$(4.9)\qquad W_{pp} = V_y^2\left[R_{pp} - \frac{\partial c}{\partial p} + (C - R_p - S_1)\frac{\partial c}{\partial y}\right] + V_{yy}^2(R_p + S_1 - C)^2\ .$$

Differentiating (4.7)

$$(4.10)\qquad R_p = F^1(K_1, L_1^*) \equiv x_1$$

$$R_{pp} = F_L^1 \frac{dL_1^*}{dp} = \frac{dx_1}{dp} .$$

Thus

$$(4.11)\qquad W_{pp} = V_y^2\left[\left(\frac{\partial x}{\partial p} - \frac{\partial c}{\partial p}\right) - (x_1 + s_1 - c_1)\frac{\partial c}{\partial y}\right] + V_{yy}^2(x+s\ \ -c)^2$$

from which we may deduce

Proposition 23. Increased uncertainty in the relative price of commodity 1 is more likely to increase expected utility (a) the larger the price elasticities of supply and demand of commodity 1, (b) the larger the income elasticity of demand if commodity 1 has positive income elasticity of demand and is imported, (c) the smaller the level of trade and (d) the smaller the degree of risk aversion.

This regime is a special case of that considered in Section C of Part I in which both consumption and production are *ex post* controls. When labor is flexible but capital fixed substitutability in production depends on the productivity of labor and its elasticity. Differentiating expression (4.5) with respect to p and substituting the expression for dL_1^*/dp into expression (4.10) indicates the short-run supply elasticity of commodity 1 is

$$(4.12)\qquad \frac{dx_1}{dp} = \frac{-(F_L^1)^2}{pF_{LL}^1 + F_{LL}^2}$$

which is greater the larger the marginal product of labor in sector 1 and the smaller the rate of diminution of the marginal product of labor in either sector.

Two implications of this result for the choice of technology under price uncertainty are that: (a) a pair of production technologies characterized by a higher degree of factor substitutability will yield a higher level of expected revenue than another pair equally productive at the expected price; and (b) a pair of production technologies for which the marginal product of the mobile factor is greater at the expected price will yield a higher level of expected revenue than another technology equally productive at the expected price. In summary, technologies intensive in the mobile factor and characterized by a high elasticity of substitution are made increasingly desirable under price uncertainty.

B. Optimal Investment and Reserve Levels

We now consider the effect of a mean-preserving spread in the distribution function $f(p)$ on optimal investment and reserve levels. Analysis of the general case becomes regrettably unwieldy and in this section and again in Section C we make some special assumptions about the form of the productive process. Here we assume that

$$(5.1) \qquad F^1(K_1, L_1) = K_1^{\alpha} L_1^{1-\alpha}, \quad 0 < \alpha < 1$$

and

$$F^2(K_2, L_2) = L_2 .$$

The production technology of commodity 1 is Cobb-Douglas with both capital and labor inputs while commodity 2 is produced only by labor at constant returns to scale. In addition we assume that only 1 reserve asset, fixed in terms of the price of commodity 2, is available.

A first-order condition for a maximum implies that the allocation of labor satisfy

$$(5.2) \qquad L_1 = p^{1/\alpha} K(1-\alpha)^{1/\alpha} .$$

Substitution of expression (5.2) into (5.1) implies that the value of output is

$$(5.3) \qquad R(K,p) = L + p^{1/\alpha} K\theta$$

where $\theta = \alpha(1-\alpha)^{(1-\alpha)/\alpha}$.

Investment, K , and the reserve level, S, are chosen to maximize

(5.4) $$E[W(K,S)] = V^1(q^1 - K - S) + E\{V^2[R(K,p) + S,\ p]\}\ .$$

To simplify the analysis we henceforth assume that commodity 1 is produced and exported but not consumed; i.e., utility only depends on revenue in terms of commodity 2's price.

First-order conditions for a maximum are given by

(5.5) $$-V_y^1 + E[V_y^2 R_K] = 0$$

$$-V_y^1 + E[V_y^2] = 0\ .$$

The effect of increased price uncertainty in the form of a mean preserving spread in $f(p)$ on optimal investment is given by the sign of

(5.6) $$-\bar{W}_{SS} W_{Kpp} + \bar{W}_{SK} W_{Spp}\ .$$

Evaluating these partial derivatives indicates

(5.7) $$W_{SS} = V_{yy}^1 + V_{yy}^2$$

$$W_{SK} = V_{yy}^1 + V_{yy}^2 R_K$$

$$W_{Kpp} = V_y^2 R_{Kpp} + V_{yy}^2 (2R_{Kp} R_p + R_K R_{pp}) + V_{yyy}^2 R_K R_p^2$$

$$W_{spp} = V_{yy}^2 R_{pp} + V_{yyy}^2 R_p^2\ .$$

If the initial situation is one of certainty the first-order conditions (5.5) imply $R_K = 1$, so that

$$\bar{W}_{SS} = \bar{W}_{SK} = V_{yy}^1 + V_{yy}^2\ .$$

In this case expression (5.6) has the sign of

(5.8) $$V_y^2 R_{Kpp} + V_{yy}^2 (2R_{Kp}R_p) \ .$$

Under the revenue function implied by the technology assumed in (5.1)

(5.9) $$R_K = p^{1/\alpha}\theta$$

$$R_p = \frac{1}{\alpha} p^{\frac{1-\alpha}{\alpha}} K\theta$$

$$R_{pp} = \frac{1-\alpha}{\alpha^2} p^{\frac{1-2\alpha}{\alpha}} K\theta$$

$$R_{Kp} = \frac{1}{\alpha} p^{\frac{1-\alpha}{\alpha}} \theta$$

$$R_{Kpp} = \frac{1-\alpha}{\alpha^2} p^{\frac{1-2\alpha}{\alpha}} \theta \ .$$

Substituting into (5.8) yields the expression

(5.10) $$\frac{\theta}{\alpha^2} p^{\frac{1}{\alpha} - 2} [V_y^2(1-\alpha) + 2V_{yy}^2 p^{1/\alpha} \theta K] \ .$$

The terms outside the parentheses are all positive. From (5.1) and (5.2) the optimal production of commodity 1 is given by

(5.11) $$x_1 = p^{\frac{1}{\alpha} - 1} K(1-\alpha)^{\frac{1}{\alpha}} \ .$$

The price elasticity of supply is

(5.12) $$\left(\frac{dx_1}{dp}\right) \frac{p}{x_1} = \frac{1-\alpha}{\alpha} = Z_s$$

while the value of output is

$$(5.13) \qquad px_1 = p^{1/\alpha} K(1-\alpha)^{1/\alpha} .$$

Expression (5.10), dividing through by αV_y , has the same sign as

$$(5.14) \qquad \frac{1-\alpha}{\alpha} + 2px_1 V_{yy}^2 / V_y$$

or, if y is total expenditure on commodity 2 consumption and $\gamma = -V_{yy}^2 y / V_y^2$, the Arrow-Pratt measure of relative risk aversion,

$$(5.15) \qquad z_s - 2\left(\frac{px_1}{y}\right)\gamma .$$

From this result we may deduce

Proposition 24. When the exported commodity employs capital in production introducing export price uncertainty increases optimal investment in the export production process if the price elasticity of supply of exports is greater than twice the product of the share of export revenue in consumption expenditure and the degree of relative risk aversion. If the price elasticity of supply is less than twice this product optimal investment is lowered by increased uncertainty.

The effect of increased price uncertainty on optimal reserve holdings is given by the sign of

$$(5.16) \qquad -\bar{W}_{KK} W_{Spp} + \bar{W}_{SK} W_{Kpp} .$$

Differentiating (5.4)

$$(5.17) \qquad W_{KK} = V_{yy}^1 + V_{yy}^2 (R_K)^2 + V_y^2 R_{KK} .$$

Initial certainty implies $R_K = 1$, while by assumption 5.1 about the underlying technology

$$(5.18) \qquad R_{KK} = 0 .$$

Expression (5.16) then has the same sign as

$$(5.19) \qquad -[V_y^2 R_{Kpp} + 2V_{yy}^2 (R_{Kp} R_p)]$$

which has the opposite sign of expression (5.8) giving the effect of price uncertainty on optimal investment. From this we may deduce:

<u>Proposition 25</u>. The effect of introducing export price uncertainty on the optimal foreign reserve level is of the opposite sign of the effect on optimal investment: if increased price uncertainty increases optimal investment it lowers optimal reserve holdings and conversely.

So far we have assumed that capital is employed in export production and not in the production of import-substitutes. We now consider the implications of reversing this assumption.

In this case revenue is

$$(5.20) \qquad p(L - L_2) + K^{\alpha} L_2^{1-\alpha} .$$

The first-order condition for a maximum implies

$$(5.21) \qquad L_2 = p^{-1/\alpha} K(1-\alpha)^{1/\alpha} .$$

When labor is optimally allocated the value of output is

(5.22) $$R(K,p) = pL + p^{\frac{\alpha-1}{\alpha}} K\theta$$

where, again,

$$\theta = \alpha(1-\alpha)^{\frac{1-\alpha}{\alpha}} .$$

Substituting the appropriate derivatives of (5.20) into expression (5.8) indicates that the effect of increased price uncertainty depends on the sign of

(5.23) $$p^{-\frac{1}{\alpha}-1}\left(\frac{1-\alpha}{\alpha^2}\right)\theta(V_y^2 - \alpha V_{yy}^2 px_1) .$$

The terms outside the brackets are positive, so that expression (5.23) has the same sign as

(5.24) $$1 + \alpha\left(\frac{px_1}{y}\right)\gamma$$

where

$$\gamma = -V_{yy}^2 y/V_y^2$$

the Arrow-Pratt measure of relative risk aversion. Expression (5.24) is always positive. From it we may deduce

Proposition 26. When the import substitute employs capital in production introducing export price uncertainty increases optimal investment in the import-substitute production activity.

As before

(5.24) $$R_{KK} = 0$$

and the effect of increased price uncertainty on optimal reserve holdings is of the opposite sign of its effect on optimal investment. We thus conclude

Proposition 27. When the import substitute employs capital in production introducing price uncertainty lowers optimal reserve levels.

In both situations considered above, in which capital is employed alternatively in the export and import-substitute sector, increased investment increases the *ex post* flexibility of the production sector by increasing the potential productivity of labor in the capital-using sector. Observe that, for the case in which capital is employed in the export sector

$$(5.25) \qquad \frac{dx_1}{dp} = \left(\frac{1}{\alpha} - 1\right)p^{\frac{1}{\alpha} - 2} K(1-\alpha)^{\frac{1}{\alpha}}$$

$$\frac{dx_2}{dp} = -\frac{1}{\alpha} p^{\frac{1}{\alpha} - 1} K(1-\alpha)^{\frac{1}{\alpha}},$$

and for the case in which capital is employed in the import-substitute sector

$$(5.26) \qquad \frac{dx_1}{dp} = \frac{1}{\alpha} p^{\frac{1}{\alpha} - 1} K(1-\alpha)^{\frac{1}{\alpha}}$$

$$\frac{dx_2}{dp} = \left(1 - \frac{1}{\alpha}\right)p^{-\frac{1}{\alpha}} K(1-\alpha)^{\frac{1}{\alpha}}.$$

In each case the absolute magnitude of the supply response coefficient is an increasing function of investment.

Increased *ex post* flexibility in production is obviously an appropriate response to increased price uncertainty. When the export sector employs capital, however, increased investment implies increased variation in the value of total production. In the presence of risk aversion this effect tends to reduce optimal investment in the export sector. When the share of export revenue in the value of total production is large and when risk aversion is significant the response of optimal investment to increased price uncertainty is likely to be negative.

When the import-substitute sector employs capital, however, increased investment reduces the sensitivity of income to export price variation. In this case risk-aversion augments the tendency for increased price uncertainty to increase optimal investment.

Reserves serve as an alternative asset whose value under assumptions made here, is not uncertain in terms of the consumed good. Increased reserve holdings do not, in contrast with increased capital holdings, increase the *ex post* flexibility of production. When increased price uncertainty reduces optimal investment in the export sector increased reserve holdings are required as a safer store of value. Conversely when increased price uncertainty leads to higher levels of investment as a means of increasing flexibility lower reserve levels are called for.

C. Optimal Specialization under Price Uncertainty

Section B considered optimal investment in export and input-substitute production activities when capital is a factor specific to the particular sector. We now consider the case in which capital is employed in both sectors and consider the problem of the *ex ante* allocation of a *given* stock of capital between the two sectors when the relative price of the export commodity is uncertain.

As with the model in Section B a general analysis is sufficiently intractable to warrant consideration of a special case.

Specifically we consider a neo-Ricardian model of specialization in which the technologies of export and import substitute production are the same, Cobb-Douglas with capital share α. Total revenue may be written as

$$(6.1) \qquad y \equiv p(\lambda K)^{\alpha} L_1^{1-\alpha} + [(1-\lambda)K]^{\alpha} L_2^{1-\alpha}$$

subject to $L_1 + L_2 \leq L$. The problem considered is the optimal *ex ante* allocation of the given capital stock K between sectors when labor is mobile *ex post*.

In analyzing a one-factor Ricardian model of export price uncertainty in which a single factor must be allocated *ex ante* between activities Turnovsky [1974] derives the following proposition:

> Suppose a risk-neutral country specializes in commodity 1 under certainty. Then under uncertainty in terms of trade it will continue to specialize completely in one but not necessarily the same commodity. If the price uncertainty is sufficiently large it may be induced to switch its specialization to commodity 2. [p. 211]

In subsequent discussion he states that "...typically, one would expect the case of risk aversion to lead to an interior solution...and consequently incomplete specialization. Unfortunately, specific tractable examples permitting us to investigate these interior solutions are extremely difficult to construct." [p. 213]

In this section we develop an example to illustrate the following result:

Proposition 28. If an export and import substitute are produced by two factors of production, one of which must be allocated between activities *ex ante* while allocation of the other may occur *ex post*, incomplete specialization may occur under price uncertainty even when complete specialization is always optimal under certainty. This result may occur even when preferences are characterized by risk neutrality.

The economy chooses a proportion of its capital stock λ to invest in the export sector to maximize the expected value of utility, a function of the value of output and the relative price of the export commodity

$$E[V(y,p)] \tag{6.2}$$

where y is defined in expression (6.1). We will assume, for simplicity, that the export commodity is not consumed. We thus suppress the second argument of V^2 .

The first-order condition for the optimal *ex post* allocation of labor implies

$$L_1/L = p^{1/\alpha}\lambda/(1-\lambda + p^{1/\alpha}\lambda) \tag{6.3}$$

which is always contained in $[0,1]$ for $\lambda \in [0,1]$. Substituting (6.3) into (6.1) yields, with some manipulation, the revenue function

$$(6.4) \qquad R(\lambda,p) = K^{\alpha}L^{1-\alpha}(1-\lambda+p^{1/\alpha}\lambda)^{\alpha} .$$

A first-order condition for a maximum is

$$(6.5) \qquad E[V_y^2 R_\lambda] \begin{cases} = 0 , & \lambda^* \in (0,1) \\ > 0 , & \lambda^* = 1 \\ < 0 , & \lambda^* = 0 . \end{cases}$$

In the case of risk neutrality or constant marginal utility of income V_y is a constant and (6.5) reduces to

$$(6.6) \qquad E[R_\lambda] = 0 .$$

Differentiating (6.4) with respect to λ

$$(6.7) \qquad R_\lambda = \alpha K^{\alpha}L^{1-\alpha}(p^{1/\alpha}-1)[(p^{1/\alpha}-1)\lambda+1]^{\alpha-1} .$$

The first three terms are positive constants so that the optimal value λ^* under risk neutrality is given by

$$(6.8) \qquad E\{(p^{1/\alpha}-1)[(p^{1/\alpha}-1)\lambda+1]^{\alpha-1}\} \begin{cases} = 0 , & \lambda^* \in (0,1) \\ > 0 , & \lambda^* = 1 \\ < 0 , & \lambda^* = 0 . \end{cases}$$

We observe that expression (6.8) does not provide an interior solution under certainty. For $p > 1$, $\lambda = 1$, and for $p < 1$, $\lambda = 0$. For $p = 0$ the solution is indeterminate.

We now demonstrate that condition (6.8) may yield an interior solution under uncertainty. We perform the change of variable

$$(6.9) \qquad x = p^{1/\alpha}$$

where

$$\ln x \sim N(\mu, \sigma^2) .$$

We define

$$(6.10) \qquad \bar{x} = \mu - \frac{1}{2}\sigma^2$$

$$(6.11) \qquad \sigma_x^2 = x^2\sigma^2 .$$

By a Taylor series expansion expression (6.8) may be written as:

$$(6.12) \qquad (\bar{x}-1)[(\bar{x}-1)\lambda + 1]^{\alpha-1} + \frac{1}{2}\lambda(\alpha-1)[1+\lambda(\bar{x}-1)]^{\alpha-3}[2+\alpha\lambda(\bar{x}-1)]\sigma_x^2 = 0$$

or, equivalently:

$$(6.13) \qquad (\bar{x}-1)[(\bar{x}-1)^2 + \frac{1}{2}(\alpha-1)\alpha\sigma_x^2]\lambda^2 + [2(\bar{x}-1)^2 + (\alpha-1)\sigma_x^2]\lambda + (\bar{x}-1) = 0 ,$$

a quadratic expression in λ .

To show that (6.13) may yield a solution for λ in $(0,1)$ consider the example

$$(6.14) \qquad \bar{x} = 2 , \quad \alpha = 1/2 , \quad \sigma^2 = 2$$

for which (6.13) has the solution

$$(6.15) \qquad \lambda = 1/2 .$$

To confirm that $\lambda = 1/2$ is an optimum we observe that expected revenue, given by

$$(6.16) \qquad K^{\alpha}L^{1-\alpha}\{[(\bar{x}-1)\lambda+1]^{\alpha} + \frac{1}{2}\,\bar{x}^{2}\alpha(\alpha-1)\lambda^{2}[(\bar{x}-1)\lambda+1]^{\alpha-2}\sigma^{2}\}$$

has value

$$(6.17) \qquad \begin{aligned} &1.089\cdot K^{\alpha}L^{1-\alpha}, \quad \text{if } \lambda = 1/2 \\ &1.0 \quad \cdot K^{\alpha}L^{1-\alpha}, \quad \text{if } \lambda = 0 \\ &1.060\cdot K^{\alpha}L^{1-\alpha}, \quad \text{if } \lambda = 1 . \end{aligned}$$

This example demonstrates the validity of Proposition 28, that a diversified investment program may be optimal when *ex post* allocation of labor is possible. It is well known that a diversified portfolio may be optimal for individuals when rates of return are uncertain and tastes are characterized by risk aversion. The optimal portfolio for a single risk-neutral investor, however, will contain only the asset with highest expected return in positive amount. Proposition 25 illustrates that when uncertainty in the rate return on capital is generated by uncertainty in future relative prices a diversified investment portfolio may yield a higher expected return when other factors are mobile between production activities. In terms of our example, when the price of commodity 1 is low, labor is transferred from production of commodity 1 to production of commodity 2. The capital invested in the production of commodity 2 is used more intensively when its price is high and conversely. The *ex post* flexibility of the economy is increased by *ex ante* diversification of immobile factors under the neoclassical assumption of smooth substitutability of factors in production activities.

Figure 2.2 depicts the result of Proposition 25. The straight line AA represents the <u>ex ante</u> production possibility frontier drawn with the assumption of mobility of both factors. We assume its slope is -1. The <u>ex post</u> production possibility frontier for a particular diversified capital structure is depicted by BB. It is tangent to AA when the marginal product of labor is equal in each sector and elsewhere lies inside AA. The ray OA represents the production possibility locus when all capital is invested in the production of commodity 1.

The relative price p of commodity 1 is p_1 with probability 1/2 and $p_2 > p_1$ with probability 1/2 where $\frac{1}{2}p_1 + \frac{1}{2}p_2 = \bar{p} > 1$. For $1 < p_1$ allocation of all capital to commodity 1 production is clearly optimal. If $p_1 < 1 < p_2$ complete specialization of investment may be suboptimal. The segment P_2P_2 represents the consumption possibility frontier when $p = p_2$ under complete specialization of capital. In this case consumption occurs at U_4. Segment P_1P_1 and point U_1 represent the consumption possibility frontier and consumption point if $p = p_1$ under complete specialization. Similarly $P_2'P_2'$ and $P_1'P_1'$ represent the consumption possibility frontiers for $p = p_2$ and $p = p_1$ respectively under incomplete specialization with accompanying consumption bundles of U_3 and U_2. If

$$\frac{1}{2}u(U_4) + \frac{1}{2}u(U_1) \leq \frac{1}{2}u(U_2) + \frac{1}{2}u(U_3)$$

incomplete specialization of investment is preferred.

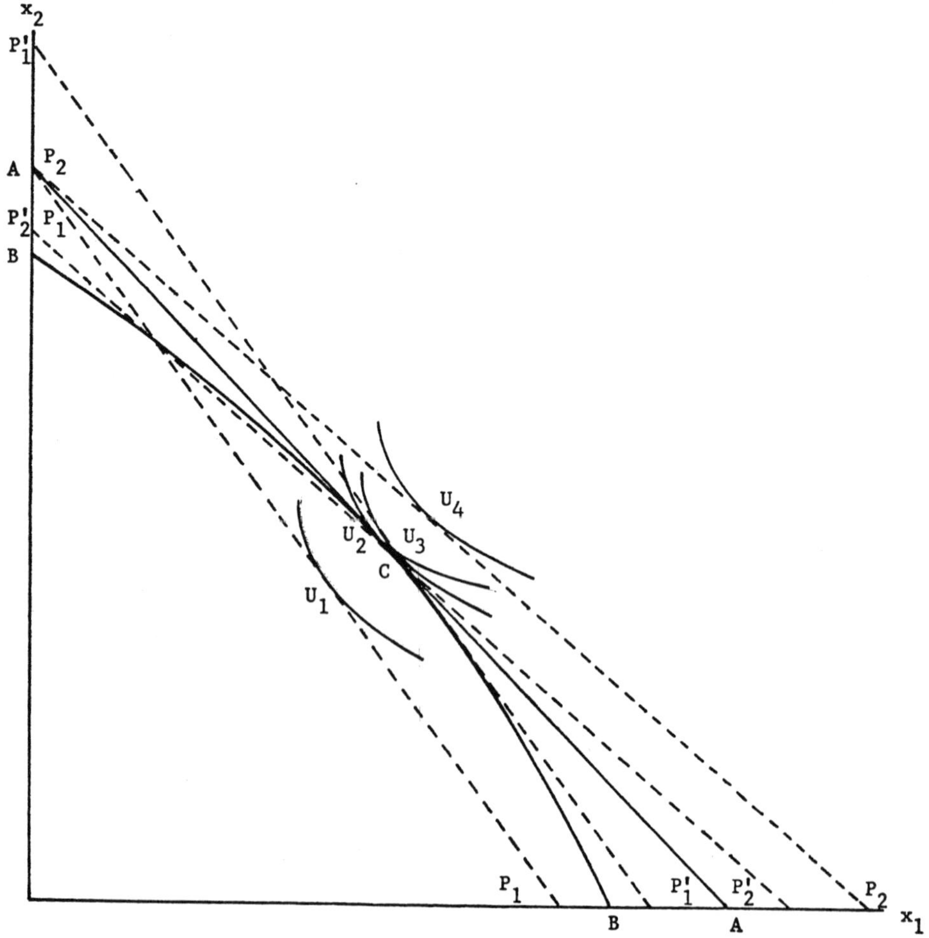

FIGURE 2.2

III. Conclusions

This essay has considered the effect of increased terms-of-trade and technological uncertainty on welfare, optimal investment and optimal foreign reserve holdings under three different assumptions about the order in which production and consumption decisions and knowledge of outcomes occur. A general result is that the greater the *ex post* flexibility in consumption and production the less likely is increased uncertainty to lower expected welfare and to raise optimal reserve holdings.

Unless the government takes steps to isolate domestic price movements from variation in world prices, it seems that the assumption that consumption allocation decisions precede knowledge of the terms of trade is inappropriate to a market economy in which individual consumers determine overall demands on the basis of observed prices. This assumption may be more appropriate to a centrally-planned economy in which exports and possibly imports are determined by yearly quotas. Perhaps the inability of centrally-planned economies to respond flexibly to movements in the terms of trade partly explains the apparent preference of these societies for autarkic development.

The *ex post* responsiveness of production decisions to international price movements and technological changes is less apparent. Clearly some factors, such as labor, are more mobile than others, such as capital. Part II of this essay has demonstrated that increased investment increases the *ex post* flexibility of the economy by increasing the productivity of the mobile factor, labor. Perhaps one would observe higher capital-labor ratios in industries among which *ex post* mobility is desirable. Capital-labor ratios in the tradable-goods sector do indeed seem to be higher than in the production of domestic goods.

REFERENCES

[1] Batra, R. N. [1975] The Pure Theory of International Trade Under Uncertainty. London: MacMillan Press.

[2] ________ and Russell [1974] "Gains from Trade Under Uncertainty," American Economic Review, 64, pp. 1040-1048.

[3] Berry, R. A. and S. H. Hymer [1969] "A Note on the Capacity to Transform and the Welfare Costs of Foreign Trade Fluctuations," Economic Journal, 79, pp. 833-846.

[4] Brainard, W. C. and R. N. Cooper [1968] "Uncertainty and Diversification in International Trade," Studies in Agricultural Economics and Development, 8, Food Research Institute, Stanford University, pp. 257-285.

[5] Leland, H. E. [1968] "Savings and Uncertainty: The Precautionary Demand for Saving," Quarterly Journal of Economics, 82, pp. 465-473.

[6] McCabe, J. L. and D. S. Sibley [1975] "Optimal Foreign Debt Accumulation with Export Revenue Uncertainty," International Economic Review (forthcoming).

[7] Nsouli, S. M. [1975] "Theoretical Aspects of Trade, Risk and Growth," Journal of International Economics, 5, pp. 239-253.

[8] Rothschild, M. and J. E. Stiglitz [1970] "Increasing Risk: I. A Definition," Journal of Economic Theory, 2, pp. 225-243.

[9] Turnovsky, S. J. [1974] "Technological and Price Uncertainty in a Ricardian Model of International Trade," Review of Economic Studies, 41, pp. 201-217.

ESSAY IV

STOCHASTIC PRODUCTION AND WEALTH EFFECTS IN A MODEL OF MONEY AND GROWTH

I. Introduction

This essay is concerned with the incorporation of both stochastic production and a savings function with wealth as an argument into the standard model of money and economic growth.

Tobin [1966] has demonstrated that the presence of outside money in the form of government debt is not neutral in a fully-employed growing economy. Specifically he shows that the equilibrium output-capital ratio of a monetary economy would be higher than that of a nonmonetary economy with the same production function, intrinsic rate of growth and savings propensity. The presence of an alternative to capital, government debt, as a form of wealth implies that some savings is syphoned away from capital accumulation. The amount that is diverted from capital formation depends on the demand for debt which depends in turn on the relative rates of return of the two assets. Government finance policy, by affecting the returns on money and capital, thus affects the equilibrium output-capital ratio of the economy; other things constant a more inflationary finance policy lowers the output-capital ratio of the economy by lowering the demand for money.

Earlier analysis of Tobin [1956] posits that the demand for money can be interpreted in part at least as behavior toward risk. Models of money and economic growth developed so far have not included any source of stochastic disturbances. Nonmonetary stochastic growth models have, however, been developed by Mirrlees [1971], Brock and Mirman [1972], Mirman [1973], Bourgignon [1974] and Merton [1975]. The last two authors demonstrate that introducing uncertainty into the rate of growth of the effective labor force lowers the expected output-capital ratio in steady state.

Section II of this essay develops a model of money and growth in which there is a stochastic term in the production function rather than in the rate of labor-supply growth. In this section both the propensity to save out of disposable income and the demand for money as a share of wealth are treated as parameters. It is demonstrated that the introduction of a stochastic term of the type assumed here raises rather than lowers the expected output-capital ratio. This result obtains for the nonmonetary as well as the monetary case. When output is random so is disposable income and investment. If investment is variable the expected marginal product of capital is not equal at all moments of time. A given average amount of savings over time will thus be less productively employed than otherwise.

It is furthermore demonstrated that increases in the savings propensity and decreases in the demand for money do not necessarily lower the expected output-capital ratio in steady state as they do in the deterministic case. Higher savings and lower demand for money tend to increase the variance of investment as well as its expected value. If the second effect dominates the first a perverse result will arise.

The theory of dynamic utility maximization indicates that not only uncertainty but the level of wealth will influence savings and portfolio decisions. Recently Blinder and Solow [1974] and Tobin and Buiter [1975] have demonstrated that when wealth effects are present in the consumption and investment functions many of the policy prescriptions of the standard IS-LM model may be reversed in the long run when stocks are endogenous. Foley and Sidrauski [1971] show that introducing wealth effects into their model of monetary and fiscal policy in a fully-employed growing economy does not effect their qualitative comparative steady-state results. They consider wealth effects only in the context of a zero-inflation policy, however.

Section III of this essay introduces a particular form of consumption behavior incorporating wealth effects into the monetary growth model. In Part A of this section a deterministic model is developed in which all labor income and a certain portion of wealth are spent on consumption.

The demand for money is assumed to respond to the rate of inflation and the capital-labor ratio. It is shown that the presence of wealth effects may disturb many of the comparative steady-state propositions of the money and growth model when the inflation rate is allowed to vary. An increase in the level of government expenditure or rate of taxation of capital income may raise both the equilibrium rate of inflation and capital-labor ratio, for instance.

Part B of this section introduces a stochastic element into the production function of the model developed in Part A. Optimizing savings and portfolio behavior under a restricted set of assumptions is incorporated into the model. It is demonstrated that in this context increased uncertainty may lower the expected output-capital ratio when savings and portfolio parameters are flexible.

II. Fiscal and Monetary Policy, Inflation and Growth in a Stochastic Economy

Tobin [1965] and Foley and Sidrauski [1971] have analyzed the effect of alternative tax, expenditure and debt policies on the steady state of a growing monetary economy. This section develops an alternative model of money and growth in which there is uncertainty in net output or in the rate of depreciation of capital. The purpose of this analysis is to consider the effect of this technological uncertainty on the rates of return of money and capital and on the steady-state distributions of output and capital per worker. Similar to the models of Feldstein [1975] and Green and Sheshinsky [1975] this model considers the effects of inflation on nominal interest rates and the taxation of income from capital.

It is found in Part B that increased uncertainty in the rate of depreciation reduces the expected value of the capital-labor and output-labor ratios and increases the expected output-capital ratio. Fiscal policies which offset the effect of uncertainty on these magnitudes are derived here. It is found that the effect of an increase in the savings rate or in the demand for real money balances on the expected output-capital ratio is ambiguous. This contradicts the result found in previous deterministic models that increased savings reduces and increased money demand increases the steady-state output-capital ratio.

Government expenditure policy determines the extent to which variation in net output is reflected by variation in disposable income. Government finance policy, however, affects the distribution of variation in disposable income between variation in the return on capital and in the rate of inflation. This is discussed in Part C.

A. The Model

Assumption 2.1(a). The production function is Cobb-Douglas:

$$(2.1a) \qquad F(K,L) = K^{\alpha}L^{1-\alpha}dt \ ; \quad f(k) = k^{\alpha}$$

where $k = K/L$ and $\alpha \in (0,1)$.

Assumption 2.2(a). Depreciation of capital K is a diffusion process of the form

$$(2.2a) \qquad \delta K dt + \sigma K dz$$

where $\delta \in [0,1)$, $\sigma \in [0,\infty)$ and dz is a standard Wiener process.

It is equivalent for the purpose of this model to assume that the production function contains a random term proportional to the capital stock. One may alternatively make

Assumption 2.1(b). The production function is of the form

$$(2.1b) \qquad F(K,L) = K^{\alpha}L^{1-\alpha}dt - \sigma K dz \ ;$$

$$f(k) = k^{\alpha}dt - \sigma k dz \ ;$$

and

Assumption 2.2(b). Depreciation of capital is a non-stochastic process of the form

$$(2.2b) \qquad \delta K dt \ .$$

In either case net output is gross output less depreciation.

Assumption 2.3. The effective labor force L grows exponentially at rate n :

$$(2.3) \qquad dL = nLdt \ , \quad n > 0 \ .$$

Equilibrium in the capital market requires that the nominal rate of return on capital equal the real rate of return plus the anticipated rate of inflation. It might be more realistic to assume that the anticipated rate of inflation equal the non-stochastic part of the inflation process. The assumption of myopic perfect foresight, that the instantaneous percentage change the price level is anticipated in the determination of the nominal interest rate, is analytically more convenient, however. This is equivalent to assuming that the return on capital is "indexed" to compensate for price level changes. Thus

Assumption 2.4. The nominal rate of return on capital r_K^n is the net marginal product of capital plus the rate of increase of the price of commodities in terms of money:

$$(2.4) \qquad r_K^n = (F_K - \delta)dt - \sigma dz + \frac{dp}{p} \ .$$

Assumption 2.5. Real income tax revenue T_I is a fixed proportion t of real wage income and the expected nominal return on capital plus a fixed proportion t' of the random return on capital, i.e.,

$$(2.5) \qquad T_I = twLdt + t\left[(F_K - \delta)dt + \frac{dp}{p}\right]K - t'\sigma dz$$

where

(2.6) $$wL = F(K,L) - (F_K - \delta)K$$

and where $t, t' \in [0,1]$.

A separate tax rate for random variations in capital depreciation is introduced to consider the effect of government participation in the risk market through partial insurance of risky undertakings. Observe that the tax rate t' applies only to the stochastic part of the real rate of return on capital. Random fluctuations in the nominal return on capital due to random variations in the rate of inflation are taxed at rate t . Similarly

Assumption 2.6. Government expenditure is a fixed proportion g of expected net output and a fixed proportion g' of the random component of output

(2.7) $$G = g(F(K,L) - \delta K)dt - g'\sigma K dz \text{ .}$$

The parameters t and g are referred to respectively as the average tax and expenditure rates and t' and g' as the marginal tax and expenditure rates.

Assumption 2.7. Real revenue from the capital gains tax T_{cg} is a fixed proportion t_{cg} of the increase in the nominal value of the capital stock:

(2.8) $$T_{cg} = t_{cg} K \frac{dp}{p} , \quad t_{cg} \in [-t,1] \text{ .}$$

Assumption 2.8. The real government deficit is financed by monetary issue:

(2.9) $$G - T_I - T_{CG} = \frac{dM}{p} \text{ .}$$

All government debt is monetary.

Definition 2.1. Net disposable real income Y_D is after tax wage and real capital income plus the change in the real value of government debt, i.e.,

$$(2.10) \qquad Y_D \equiv (wL + r_K K - G) + d\left(\frac{M}{p}\right).$$

Definition 2.2. Real wealth W is composed of real money balances plus the capital stock:

$$(2.11) \qquad W \equiv \frac{M}{p} + K .$$

Assumption 2.9. Real net savings is a fixed proportion s of net disposable real income:

$$(2.12) \qquad dW = sY_D , \quad s \in [0,1] .$$

Assumption 2.10. The demand for real monetary balances is a fixed proportion m of the capital stock:

$$(2.13) \qquad \left(\frac{M}{p}\right)^d = mK , \quad m \geq 0 .$$

Assumption 2.11. The price of commodities in terms of money is perfectly flexible; desired and actual real money balances are always equal:

$$(2.14) \qquad p = \frac{M}{mK} .$$

Assumptions 2.1 through 2.11 determine the dynamic behavior of capital, output and the price level. Section B derives the equation of motion for the capital-labor ratio and considers the effect of changes in uncertainty, government policy and savings and portfolio behavior on the expected output-capital ratio of the economy in steady state. The dynamic behavior of the price level is considered in Section C.

B. Output, Capital and Uncertainty

Substituting (2.6), (2.10) and (2.13) into (2.12) provides an expression for the change in capital stock:

$$(2.15) \qquad dK = \frac{s}{\rho}\left[(1-g)(F - \delta K)dt - (1-g')\sigma K dz\right]$$

where

$$\rho = 1 + m(1-s) \ .$$

Applying Itô's lemma to differentiate $k \equiv K/L$ yields

$$(2.16) \qquad dk = [(s/\rho)(1-g)(k^{\alpha} - \delta k) - nk]dt - (s/\rho)(1-g')\sigma k dz$$

$$= (b_1 k^{\alpha} - b_2 k)dt + a^{1/2} k dz$$

where

$$b_1 = (s/\rho)(1-g) > 0$$

$$b_2 = n + \delta b_1 \quad > 0$$

and

$$a^{1/2} = s(1-g')\sigma/\rho \ .$$

Proposition 2.1. For constant values of the savings parameter (s) and the demand for money parameter (m) the distribution of the capital-labor ratio is independent of the source of finance of government expenditure or the rate of inflation.

Equation (2.16), the equation of motion for k , does not contain the variables t , t' or p . The rate of capital accumulation depends only on disposable income and the savings and asset demand parameters. If the last two are constant government policy affects the rate of capital accumulation only through its affect on disposable income. By Assumptions 2.10 and 2.11 the capital gains component of disposable income depends only on the rate of capital accumulation. Hence policy affects income only through expenditure.

Theorem 2.1. Assumptions 2.1 through 2.11 imply the existence of a steady-state distribution for k .

Proof. Define

$$(2.17) \qquad W_1(k) \equiv \exp[-2(b_1/a)\int^k y^{\alpha-2}dy]\cdot\exp[2(b_2/a)\int^k y^{-1}dy]$$

$$= m_1 k^{c_2}\exp[c_1 k^{\alpha-1}]$$

where $c_1 = 2b_1/a(1-\alpha) > 0$ and $c_2 = 2b_2/a > 0$. Observe that $W_k(k) \notin I(0,\bar{k})$ and $W_1(k) \notin I(\bar{k},\infty)$. Similarly, define:

$$(2.18) \qquad W_2(k) = (ak^2)^{-1}\exp[2(b_1/a)\int^k y^{\alpha-2}dy]\cdot\exp[-2(b_2/a)\int^k y^{-1}dy]$$

$$= m_2 k^{-c_2-2}\exp[-c_1 k^{\alpha-1}] .$$

Again, $W_2(k) \in I(0,\infty)$. Conditions (A.7) of the Appendix imply that k is not absorbed at 0 or ∞ and hence that a steady-state distribution exists for k .

End of Proof

A steady-state distribution exists since the change in the capital-labor ratio proportional to output per worker is positive while that proportional to capital per worker is negative. The drift term in (2.15) is positive near zero for $b_1 > 0$ since output per worker is large relative to k in this region. Conversely when $-b_2 < 0$ the drift term in (2.15) is negative for very large values of k since k is large relative to output per worker in this region.

From expression (A.4) of the Appendix the existence of a steady-state distribution for k implies that k has c.d.f.:

$$\text{(2.19)} \qquad \pi(k) = mk^{-\frac{2b_2}{a} - 2} \exp[-2b_1 k^{\alpha-1}/(1-\alpha)a] \ .$$

where

$$\text{(2.20)} \qquad m = [2b_1/(1-\alpha)a]^{[2b_2/(1-\alpha)a]} \Gamma[2b_2/(1-\alpha)a]$$

where $\Gamma(x) \equiv \int_0^\infty t^{x-1} e^{-t} dt$, the gamma function. From the properties of the gamma function it can be demonstrated that:

$$\text{(2.21)} \qquad E(k) = \frac{\Gamma\left(\frac{2b_2}{(1-\alpha)a}\right)}{\Gamma\left(\frac{2b_2 + a}{(1-\alpha)a}\right)} \left[\frac{2b_1}{(1-\alpha)a}\right]^{1/1-\alpha} \ .$$

Applying Stirling's formula[1] to (2.21) yields the approximation

---

[1] Stirling's formula is

$$\Gamma(x) \sim \sqrt{2\pi}\, e^{-x} x^{x-1/2}$$

where $\sim$ implies equality in the limit as $x \to \infty$. See Feller [1968, p. 66] for this result.

$$(2.22)\qquad E(k) \sim e^{1/1-\alpha}\left(\frac{2b_2}{2b_2+a}\right)^{\left[\frac{2b_2}{(1-\alpha)a}-\frac{1}{2}\right]}[2b_1/(2b_2+a)]^{1/1-\alpha}\ .$$

The existence of a steady-state distribution for k also allows application of (A.9) to (2.16). Setting $g(k) = \log k$ yields

$$(2.23)\qquad E[k^{\alpha-1}] = b_2/b_1 + \frac{1}{2}\,a/b_1\ .$$

Observe that, in a non-monetary, deterministic economy without government, i.e. an economy in which $\alpha = t = t_{cg} = t' = g = \sigma^2 = 0$, that (2.23) reduces to

$$(2.24)\qquad k^{\alpha-1} - \delta = n/s$$

which is the Harrod-Domar equilibrium condition: that the net output-capital ratio equal the natural rate of growth divided by the savings rate.

Setting $g(k) = k$ and applying (A.9) give the relationship

$$(2.25)\qquad E[k^{\alpha}] = (b_2/b_1)E[k]\ .$$

Substituting (2.22) into (2.25) yields

$$(2.26)\qquad E[k^{\alpha}] \sim e^{1/1-\alpha}\left[\frac{2b_2}{2b_2+a}\right]^{\left[\frac{2b_2}{(1-\alpha)a}-\frac{1}{2}\right]}(b_2/b_1)[2b_1/(2b_2+a)]^{1/1-\alpha}$$

for the expected output-labor ratio.

The effects of uncertainty, of changes in policy parameters, and of changes in savings and portfolio behavior on the capital-labor, output-capital, and output-labor ratios in steady state may be analyzed with expressions (2.22), (2.23) and (2.26), respectively.

1. <u>Stochastic Output and the Steady State</u>

In general the effect of an increase in the coefficient of the random component of net output on the capital-labor ratio is ambiguous. When the variance is small, however, increased uncertainty will reduce the output-labor and capital-labor ratios.

Setting

$$h(k) = \log[E(k)]$$

and differentiating with respect to σ^2 yields

$$(2.27) \qquad (s/\rho)(1-g')^2\left\{-\left[\frac{4b_2+(1+\alpha)a}{2(1-\alpha)a(2b_2+a)}\right] - \frac{2b_2}{(1-\alpha)a^2}[\ln 2b_2 - \ln(2b_2+a)]\right\} .$$

The first term inside the ellipses is negative and the second is positive. A Taylor series expansion of $\ln 2b_2$ around $\ln(2b_2+a)$ yields the relationship

$$(2.28) \qquad [\ln 2b_2 - \ln(2b_2+a)] = \frac{-a}{2b_2+a} - \frac{a^2}{2(2b_2+a)^2} + o(a^3)$$

which when substituted into (2.27) gives

$$(2.29) \qquad \left\{\frac{-2b_2\alpha - (1+\alpha)a}{2(2b_2+a)^2(1-\alpha)} + o(a)\right\}(s/\rho)(1-g')^2$$

which is negative for small values of a .

Since

$$(2.30) \qquad E(k^{\alpha}) = (b_2/b_1)E(k)$$

the effect of an increase in uncertainty on the expected output-labor ratio is of the same sign as the effect on the capital-labor ratio. From these results one may conclude:

Proposition 2.2. An increase in the variance of the random component of net output reduces the expected capital-labor and output-labor ratios when the variance of the random component is near zero.

Expression (2.23) demonstrates:

Proposition 2.3. The expected output-capital ratio and the expected marginal productivity of capital are directly proportional to the variance in the depreciation rate.

Propositions 2.2 and 2.3 follow from the strict concavity of output per worker in the capital-labor ratio. A mean-preserving spread in the distribution of the capital-labor ratio reduces expected output per worker and, hence, capital accumulation per worker. The resulting decline in the expected rate of accumulation lowers the expected capital-labor ratio in steady state. Similarly the expected output-capital ratio and marginal productivity of capital are positively related to the variance parameter since these variables are convex functions of the capital-labor ratio.

This set of results is in contrast with the findings of Bourgignon

[1974] and Merton [1975] that increased uncertainty in the rate of labor supply growth raises the expected capital-labor ratio and reduces the expected output-labor ratio. More uncertainty in the rate of labor supply growth does increase uncertainty in the capital-labor ratio which will have the effect discussed above. The expected value of the capital-labor ratio is also increased, however, since the capital-labor ratio is itself a convex function of the labor supply. In the Bourgignon-Merton formulation this second effect dominates the first.

2. Government Expenditure and the Steady State

From (2.23) one may derive the effects of changes in the average and marginal government expenditure rates on the expected output-capital ratio in steady state. Differentiation yields

$$\frac{\partial E(k^{\alpha-1})}{\partial g} = \frac{n\rho}{s(1-g)^2} > 0 \tag{2.31}$$

and

$$\frac{\partial E(k^{\alpha-1})}{\partial g'} = \frac{-s(1-g')\sigma^2}{\rho(1-g)} < 0 \tag{2.32}$$

from which are deduced:

Proposition 2.4. An increase in the average rate of government expenditure raises the steady-state expected output-capital ratio; and

Proposition 2.5. An increase in the marginal rate of government expenditure lowers the steady-state expected output-capital ratio.

An increase in the average expenditure rate lowers expected disposable income and hence expected savings and capital accumulation while not affecting the variance in disposable income and the rate of accumulation. The effect of reduced average capital accumulation on the expected output-capital ratio is positive.

An increase in the marginal expenditure rate does not affect the expected value of disposable income for a given expected output level. It does, however, reduce the variance of disposable income for a given variance of real output. A reduction in the variance of disposable income causes less variance in the rate of capital accumulation and in the capital-labor ratio. Expected output per worker and capital accumulation per worker is consequently higher. The expected capital-labor ratio in steady state is thus greater.

Definition 2.3. Government expenditure policy is totally risk absorbing if $g' = 1$.

In this case the entire random component in net output is absorbed by government expenditure.

Proposition 2.6. If government expenditure policy is totally risk absorbing the steady-state capital-labor ratio and the disposable income level are independent of the variance in net output and equal the values they would assume in the deterministic case.

This result is evident since $a = 0$ when $g' = 1$.

3. Savings, Portfolio Behavior and the Steady State

A standard result of both non-monetary and monetary growth theory is that the equilibrium output-capital ratio and marginal productivity of capital depend negatively on the savings propensity and positively on the demand for money (Solow [1970], Tobin [1965]). In a stochastic economy the effect of changes in these parameters is ambiguous. An increase in s or decrease in m increases both the rate of capital accumulation and its variance. The first effect tends to decrease the expected output-capital ratio while the second tends to increase it. Differentiation of (2.23) with respect to s and m yields:

Proposition 2.7. An increase in s and decrease in m reduce the expected output-capital ratio if and only if

$$n \geq \frac{s^2(1-g')\sigma^2}{(1+m(1-s))} .$$

When n is small relative to σ^2 the effect of changes in s and m on the variance of the rate of capital accumulation dominate.

Proposition 2.8. At a given level of capital the mean and the variance of disposable income is an increasing function of the desired ratio of real money balances to capital, m, and of the savings rate, s.

(2.33) $$Y_D = (1-g)(F-\delta K)dt - (1-g')\sigma K dz + d(M/p) .$$

From expression (2.13) and (2.14)

(2.34) $$d(M/p) = m dK .$$

Substituting expression (2.15) into (2.34) and substituting again into (2.33) implies

$$(2.35)\qquad Y_D = [(1+m)/\rho][(1-g)(F-\delta K)dt - (1-g')\sigma K dz] \;.$$

Since $(1+m)/\rho$ is an increasing function of m and s the proposition holds.

Observe that since $(1+m)/\rho > 1$ the variance of disposable income is greater than that in output when $g' = 0$. The presence of an asset whose value is proportional to the capital stock augments uncertainty in disposable income. Variation in the capital stock creates variation in the demand for money. The consequent variation in the value of outstanding debt generates additional uncertainty through capital gains and losses.

C. Inflation, the Return on Capital and Uncertainty

Section B has discussed the effects of uncertainty, government policy and household savings and portfolio behavior on real output and the capital stock. This section considers the relationship between these technological, policy and behavioral variables on the rate of inflation and the return on capital.

Applying Itô's lemma to differentiate

$$(2.14) \qquad p = \frac{M}{mK}$$

and substituting (2.9) and (6.15) as expressions of dM and dK respectively yields

$$(2.36) \qquad \frac{dp}{p} = \frac{1}{m+t+t_{cg}}\{[g - t - (sm/\rho)(1-g)](k^{\alpha-1} - \delta)$$
$$- [s(1-g')/\rho][(g' - t') - (sm/\rho)(1-g')]\sigma^2\}dt$$
$$- \frac{1}{m+t+t_{cg}}[(g' - t') - (sm/\rho)(1-g')]\sigma dz$$

where $\rho = 1 + m(1-s)$. The rate of return on capital is given by

$$(2.37) \qquad r_K = (1-t)(\alpha k^{\alpha-k} - \delta)dt - (1-t')\sigma dz - (t+t_{cg})\frac{dp}{p} .$$

While government policy affects uncertainty in disposable income through its expenditure policy, tax policy allocates the random component of disposable income into uncertainty in the rate of return on capital and in the rate of inflation. From (2.36) one may deduce:

Proposition 2.9. The inflation rate is non-stochastic if

$$(2.38) \qquad g' - t' = (sm/\rho)(1 - g')$$

and

Proposition 2.10. The inflation rate is non-stochastic and zero if

$$(2.38) \qquad g' - t' = (sm/\rho)(1 - g')$$

and

$$(2.39) \qquad g - t = (sm/\rho)(1-g) \ .$$

The left-hand side of (2.38) represents the marginal deficit or change in money supply caused by a random movement in output. The right-hand side is the marginal demand for money or change in demand for money resulting from a random movement in output. When these are equal random movements in output do not generate random variation in inflation.

Similarly the left-hand side of (2.39) represents the average deficit or expected increase in money supply per unit of capital while the right-hand side represents the average or expected increase in the demand for money per unit of capital. If these are equal and inflation is non-stochastic the inflation rate is zero. Observe that zero inflation requires a deficit while a balanced budget is deflationary.

Proposition 2.11. An increase in the variance of the random component of output increases or decreases the expected inflation rate as

$$(g' - t') \lessgtr \frac{sm}{\rho}(1 - g') \ .$$

An increase in the variance of the demand for money tends to raise expected inflation. If the covariance between demand and supply is sufficiently negative, however, this effect is offset. These results follow from Jensen's inequality.

Definition 2.4. The inflationary bias of the revenue system is given by $t + t_{cg}$. Tax policy is inflation neutral if $t + t_{cg} = 0$.

Proposition 2.12. An increase in the inflation bias of the tax system reduces the expected absolute value of the rate of inflation and its variance.

This result is evident from inspection of expression (2.36). The inflationary bias of the tax system operates to stabilize price movements: an increase in either the non-random or random component of the inflation rate tends to increase revenue and reduce the deficit and supply of money, lowering the inflation rate. Conversely for a decrease in the inflation rate.

Propositions 2.9 through 2.12 have dealt with the effects of policy and uncertainty on inflation or the rate of return on money. The effects of policy on the return on capital and the covariance of the returns on money and capital are now considered.

Proposition 2.13. The rate of return on capital is non-stochastic if $t' = 1$ and either (1) tax policy is inflation neutral or (2) $g' = 1$.

When $t' = 1$ the government absorbs the entire amount of the variance in the marginal productivity of capital. If tax policy is inflation neutral variation in inflation does not affect the after tax return on capital. Alternatively, if $g' = t' = 1$ expenditure policy absorbs all risk and the return on both money and capital is non-stochastic.

Proposition 2.14. If tax policy is inflation neutral and $t' < 1$ then the return on capital and on money are negatively or positively correlated as

$$(g' - t') \gtrless \frac{sm}{\rho}(1 - g') \ .$$

For $t' < 1$ and $t + t_{cg} = 0$ the random component of output and the random component of the net return on capital are of the same sign. If random variations in output affect money supply more than money demand the random component of the inflation rate will be of the same sign as the random component of output (inflation will be high when output is high). The rate of return on money and capital are then of opposite sign. Conversely for the case in which random variation in output affects the demand for money more than supply.

Proposition 2.15. An inflation bias in the tax system increases the chance that the rates of return on money and capital are positively correlated.

When $t + t_{cg} > 0$ a negative movement in the rate of inflation represents both (1) a negative movement in the return on money and (2) an increase in tax obligations per unit of capital.

D. Conclusion

This section has extended the stochastic growth models of Bourgignon [1974] and Merton [1975] to include government fiscal policy as well as a monetary asset. It is shown that introducing a stochastic term in net output proportional to the capital stock lowers the expected output-labor and capital-labor ratios and raises the expected output-capital ratio.

A high marginal government expenditure rate will offset the effect of uncertainty by absorbing the random component of net output. Taxation policy determines the extent to which remaining random variation in disposable income is converted into uncertainty in the rate of return on capital and in the inflation rate.

Solow [1970] has shown that, in a deterministic growth model, higher savings reduces the output-capital ratio. Tobin [1965] has demonstrated, in a deterministic model of money and growth, that increased money demand raises the output-capital ratio. Uncertainty in net output, however, makes the effects of changes in these parameters ambiguous.

The model presented in this section has treated the savings and portfolio choice parameters as exogenous. The next section examines the implications of alternative savings and portfolio behavior by introducing wealth effects into the savings function and treating the demand for money as a function of the expected rate of inflation and rate of interest. Many of the findings of the present section do not necessarily hold under these relaxations.

III. Fiscal and Monetary Policy, Inflation and Growth with Flexible Savings and Portfolio Behavior

In two recent studies Blinder and Solow [1974] and Tobin and Buiter [1975] analyze the long-run effects of policy changes when wealth and the capital stock are endogenous. They consider the effects of alternative government policies on income and the price level in both an underemployed and fully-employed economy. Their results demonstrate that these modifications may upset many of the conclusions of standard IS-LM analysis.

Part A of this section incorporates a savings function involving wealth into a long-run model of money and growth. The effects of alternative expenditure and finance policies on the equilibrium capital-labor ratio and rate of inflation are derived. It is demonstrated that under the alternative savings formulation many of the conclusions about the effects of policy obtained from the standard model of money and growth are modified.

Part B extends this analysis to the stochastic case. The theory of savings and portfolio choice under uncertainty provides a microeconomic foundation for the savings and money demand functions assumed here. It is shown that when wealth affects saving in the way assumed and when the demand for money is interest and inflation elastic increased uncertainty may reduce the expected output-capital ratio.

A. A Deterministic Model of Money and Growth

In this section assumptions 2.1(a), 2.3, 2.6, 2.8 and 2.11 of Section II are maintained. For simplicity the rate of depreciation is assumed to be zero.

It is highly convenient to separate income of labor from the income from wealth in the analysis. For this reason a modified Cambridge savings assumption is adopted:

Assumption 3.9. All after-tax labor income is spent on consumption. Wealth holders consume a proportion c of their wealth in each period.[1]

Total private consumption in period t, $C(t)$, is therefore given by

$$(3.1) \qquad C(t) = (1-\alpha)(1-t_w)K(t)^{\alpha}L(t)^{1-\alpha} + cW(t)$$

where t_w represents the tax rate on labor income.

To replace assumption 2.10, that the demand for real money balances is a fixed proportion of the capital stock, is

Assumption 3.10. The demand for real money balances is a share $m(\pi^e + n, k)$ of the capital stock; i.e.,

$$(3.2) \qquad \left(\frac{M}{P}\right)^d = m(\pi^e + n,\ k)K\ , \quad m \geq 0$$

where π^e is the expected rate of inflation.

---

[1] If the wealth holder's utility function is of the form $u(x) = \log x$ Assumption 3.9 may be derived from the intertemporal utility maximizing behavior of the wealth holder if he has no alternative source of income. This is shown in Part B. Note that if $\gamma = 0$ in expression (3.19), $c = \delta$ where δ is the discount factor.

It is assumed that an increase in the expected rate of inflation, by lowering the anticipated return on money, lowers the demand for real money balances; i.e. $m_1 \leq 0$. When the amount of capital per worker is high the rate of return on capital is lower and the level of output is greater than otherwise. The first effect reduces the demand for capital as an asset while the second generates a transactions demand for money balances. It is therefore assumed that $m_2 \geq 0$.

On the basis of these assumptions one may derive a differential equation for the change in the capital stock

$$(3.3) \qquad \dot{K} = [1 - (1-\alpha)(1 - t_w) - g]K^{\alpha}L^{1-\alpha} - c(1+m)K$$

which, dividing through by L and then k becomes

$$(3.4) \qquad \frac{\dot{k}}{k} = [1 - (1-\alpha)(1 - t_w) - g]k^{\alpha-1} - [c(1+m) + n] .$$

Expression (3.4) defines a locus of points in $(k, \pi^e + n)$ space for which $\dot{k} = 0$, i.e., for which the system is in steady state. That this locus is an upward sloping curve may be shown by setting $\dot{k}/k = 0$ and differentiating (3.4) to obtain the relationship

$$(3.5) \qquad \frac{d\pi}{dk} = \frac{(\alpha-1)k^{\alpha-2}[1 - (1-\alpha)(1 - t_w) - g] - cm_2}{cm_1} .$$

As long as government expenditure and workers' consumption constitute less than all of output expression (3.5) is positive. When $c = 0$, when capitalists do not consume at all, or when $m_1 = 0$, when the demand for real cash balances is unaffected by the rate of inflation, expression (3.4) defines a vertical line in $(k, \pi^e + n)$ space: any rate of inflation is compatible with a given capital-labor ratio.

Taxes are collected on real income from capital at rate t_c. In the terminology of Section II it is assumed that the tax system is inflation neutral. The government budget constraint and Assumption 2.8 imply

$$\frac{\dot{M}}{p} = [g - t_w + \alpha(t_w - t_c)]F(K,L) \; . \tag{3.6}$$

Differentiating expression (3.2) with respect to time yields

$$\frac{\dot{M}}{p} - \pi\left(\frac{M}{p}\right) = m\dot{K} + (m_1\dot{\pi}^e + m_2\dot{k})K \tag{3.7}$$

or, equivalently,

$$[g - t_w + \alpha(t_w - t_c)]k^{\alpha-1} = m(\pi + n + \dot{k}/k) + m_1\dot{\pi}^e + m_2\dot{k} \; . \tag{3.8}$$

where π is the actual inflation rate. In steady state $\dot{k} = \dot{\pi}^e = 0$ and $\pi^e = \pi$ in which case expression (3.8) reduces to

$$k^{\alpha-1} = \frac{m(\pi+n)}{[g - t_w + \alpha(t_w - t_c)]} \; . \tag{3.9}$$

Expression (3.9) defines a locus of points in $(k, \pi+n)$ space for which the demand and supply of real cash balances are equal in steady state. That this locus is a curve of indeterminate sign may be demonstrated by differentiating expression (3.9) to obtain

$$\frac{d(\pi+n)}{dk} = \frac{a(\alpha-1)k^{\alpha-2} - m_2(\pi+n)}{m + m_1(\pi+n)} \tag{3.10}$$

where $a = g - t_w + \alpha(t_w - t_c)$, the deficit per unit of output. By substituting (3.9) into (3.10) and multiplying by k/m expression (3.10) may be written as

$$(3.11) \qquad \frac{(\alpha-1) - (Z_2 - 1)(\pi+n)}{1 - Z_1}$$

where

$$Z_1 = -m_1(\pi+n)/m \geq 0$$

the elasticity of the demand for real money balances with respect to the rate of inflation plus the growth rate and

$$Z_2 = 1 + m_2 k/m \geq 1$$

the elasticity of demand for real money balances with respect to the capital-labor ratio.

The numerator of expression (3.11) is always negative while the denominator is positive or negative as $Z_1 \gtrless 1$. When $Z_1 = 1$ the numerator of expression (3.9) is constant so that it defines a vertical line in $(k, \pi+n)$ space.

This relationship defines a locus of points in $(k, \pi+n)$ space of "portfolio balance" or an LM curve of sorts. By similar analogy, from expression (3.4), the relationship

$$(3.12) \qquad k^{\alpha-1} = \frac{c(1+m) + n}{1 - (1-\alpha)(1 - t_w) - g}$$

defines a locus of "real balance" or an "IS curve."

Steady states under alternative assumptions about fiscal policy and consumption behavior may be compared by analyzing the effect of changes in the appropriate parameters on the loci of points defined by expressions

(3.9) and (3.12). Four alternative assumptions about the value of the inflation elasticity of the demand for money are made.

1. Zero Inflation Elasticity of Demand for Money

In this case expression (3.12), the IS curve, is a vertical line in $(k, \pi+n)$ space while expression (3.9), the LM curve, is downward sloping since $m_1 = Z_1 = 0$. These curves are depicted in Figure 4.1.

An increase in expenditure due to a rise in g or c or a reduction in t_w at a given level of a, the deficit per unit of output, shifts the IS curve leftward. The new steady state is characterized by a lower capital-labor ratio and a higher rate of inflation. Increased expenditure lowers investment and a lower capital-labor ratio results. Since the per capita deficit is a concave function of the capital-labor ratio the percentage decline in the first is less than that in the second. Since the demand for real per capita money balances is a fixed proportion of the capital stock the flow of new real cash balances supplied exceeds the flow demanded at the original rate of inflation and lower capital-labor ratio. At the new equilibrium the rate of inflation is therefore greater.

An increase in the tax rate on capital income, t_c, shifts the LM curve, expression (3.9), downward. The capital-labor ratio is unchanged but the rate of inflation is lower. Since the tax increase does not affect consumption or government expenditure the capital-labor ratio is unaffected. The reduction in the deficit reduces the supply of new money balances at the margin but the demand is unchanged at the original rate of inflation. For this reason the new steady-state inflation rate is lower.

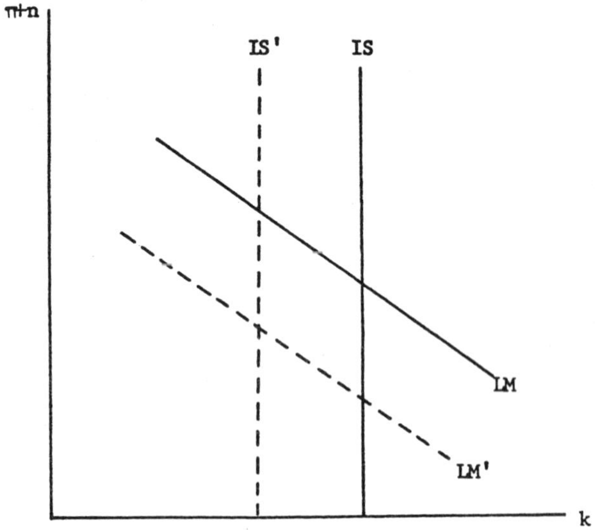

FIGURE 4.1

2. Inflation Elasticity of Demand for Money Between Zero and Unity

In this case the IS curve, expression (3.12), is upward sloping while the LM curve, expression (3.9), is downward sloping. This situation is depicted in Figure 4.2.

The qualitative effects of an increased propensity of the government or of capitalists to spend or decrease in the tax on labor income, holding the deficit per unit of output constant, remains the same as in case 1. An increase in the tax on capital income, however, now lowers the capital-labor ratio as well as the rate of inflation. The reduction in the rate of inflation at the original level of capital increases the demand for real cash balances. The consequent fall in the price level increases per capita wealth and consumption expenditure by capitalists. A lower steady-state capital-labor ratio results.

3. Unit Inflation Elasticity of Demand for Money

Here, as illustrated in Figure 4.3, the LM curve is vertical while the IS curve slopes upward. An increase in g or c or a reduction in t_w raises the inflation rate but the capital-labor ratio is unchanged. At the higher rate of inflation the demand for money is reduced, raising the price level and lowering wealth. The consequent reduction in capitalists' consumption exactly offsets the initial increase in expenditure. For the case of changes in c the Kaldorian "widow's cruse" is exactly reversed. Rather than earning more as a result of spending more out of their income, capitalists, when trying to spend more as a share of their wealth, reduce the value of their wealth to the point where their absolute spending is unchanged.

The qualitative effects of an increase in t_w are the same as

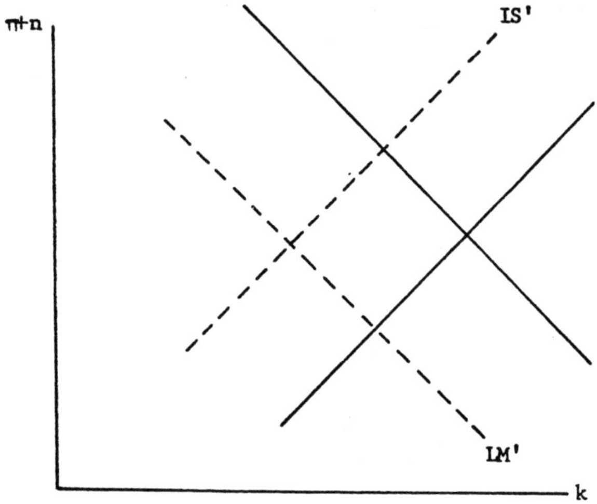

FIGURE 4.2

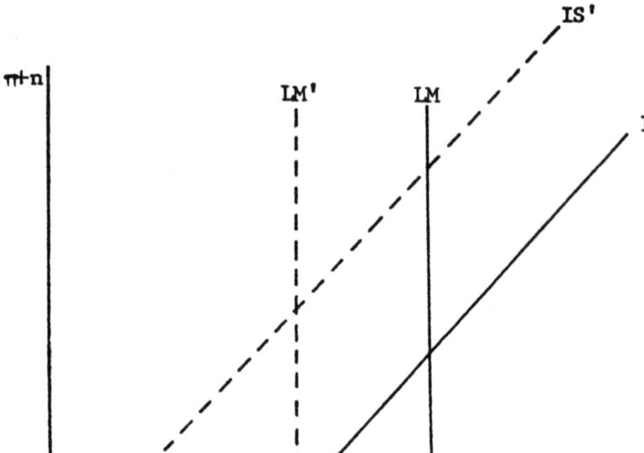

FIGURE 4.3

those derived in case 2: the LM curve shifts leftward and the capital-labor ratio and inflation rate are lower at the new equilibrium.

4. Inflation Elasticity of Demand for Money Greater than Unity

In this case both IS and LM curves are upward sloping. Two cases are to be distinguished.

a. LM Curve Steeper than IS Curve

In this case, as shown in Figure 4.4a, an increase in the propensity to spend of the government or capitalists or in the share of income received by workers increases both the rate of inflation and the capital-labor ratio. The effect of the increased inflation is to lower real cash balances to the point where capitalists' consumption is reduced by an amount greater than the original increase in expenditure.

An increase in t_c, reducing the deficit, now shifts the LM curve upward. The new equilibrium is characterized by less inflation and a lower capital-labor ratio, as in cases 2 and 3.

b. IS Curve Steeper than LM Curve

In this case, illustrated in Figure 4.4b, increased expenditure reduces both the equilibrium inflation rate and the capital-labor ratio. At the original capital-labor ratio and inflation rate, $\dot{k} < 0$. At higher rates of inflation, at the original capital-labor ratio, money is in excess supply. Increasing the capital-labor ratio increases the inflation rate necessary for real balance by more than the increase necessary to maintain portfolio balance since the inflation sensitivity of the demand for money is so large. Only at a lower capital-labor ratio and inflation rate does equilibrium obtain.

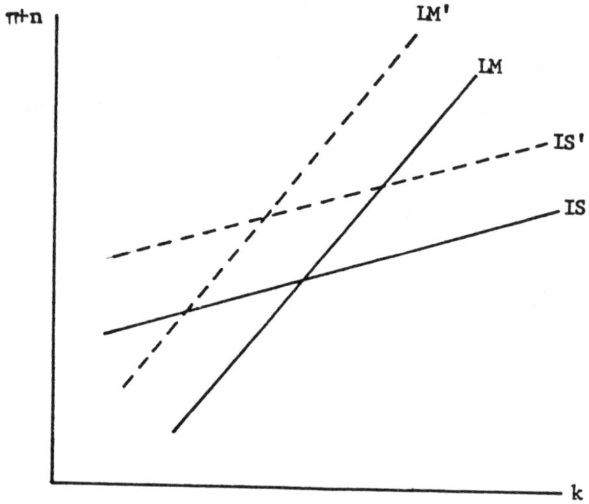

FIGURE 4.4a

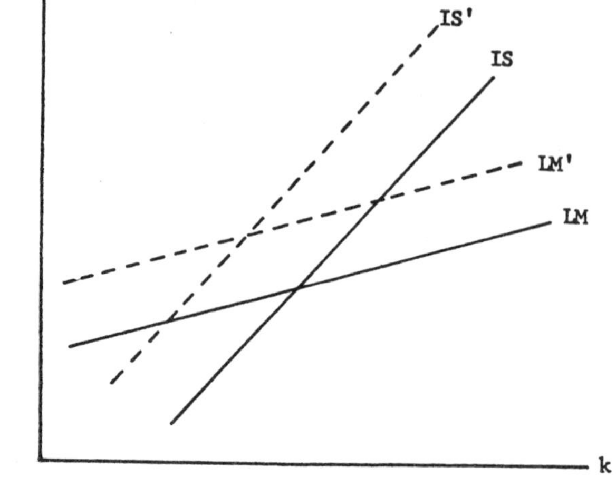

FIGURE 4.4b

An increase in t_c, reducing the deficit, again shifts the LM curve upward. The new equilibrium is characterized by a higher capital-labor ratio and inflation rate, in contrast with the previous cases considered.[2]

The results discussed above are summarized as follows:

Proposition 3.1. When either (1) consumption is independent of wealth or (2) the demand for money is independent of the rate of inflation an increase in the propensity to spend at a constant deficit per unit of output reduces the equilibrium capital-labor ratio and raises the equilibrium rate of inflation. An increase in the tax rate at a given spending propensity lowers the equilibrium rate of inflation while leaving the capital-labor ratio unaffected. When (1) consumption depends positively on wealth and (2) the demand for money depends negatively on the rate of inflation the effects of changes in either the expenditure or tax parameters may be reversed.

In an economy in which a portion of private wealth consists of public debt the level of wealth depends on the value placed on public debt by the private sector. This evaluation is an increasing function of the expected rate of return on that debt or, in the present model, on the rate of deflation.

The microeconomic foundations of the consumption-savings decision

---

[2]The above discussion is concerned solely with the comparison of steady states and makes no pretense of considering the local stability of equilibria under alternative assumptions. The problem of stability, while of critical importance, is both very messy and tangential to the problem at hand.

imply that, at a given level of income, consumption is generally an increasing function of wealth. While the class distinctions in savings behavior implied by the Cambridge savings assumptions are, no doubt, undescriptive, the approach adopted here is at least suggestive of the ability of wealth effects to modify policy prescriptions when wealth is endogenous and the inflation rate variable.

B. Savings and Portfolio Selection in a Stochastic Model of Money and Growth

Part A has assumed a fixed consumption-wealth ratio for wealth holders and a general demand for money function. The theory of portfolio choice under uncertainty provides a microeconomic foundation for savings and portfolio behavior in a stochastic environment. This part develops a stochastic version of the model presented in Part A embedding optimal portfolio and savings behavior under a restrictive set of assumptions. It is shown that, in these circumstances, increased uncertainty may raise the expected output-capital ratio, in contrast with Proposition 2.2 of Section II.

The assumptions of Part A are maintained except for the reintroduction of a stochastic component in the production function, i.e.,

Assumption 3.1'. The production function is of the form

$$F(K,L) = K^{\alpha}L^{1-\alpha}dt - \sigma K dz \; . \tag{3.13}$$

The equation of motion for the capital-labor ratio is

$$dk = \{(\alpha-\hat{g})k^{\alpha} - [c(1+m)+n]k\}dt - (1-g')\sigma k dz \tag{3.14}$$

where

$$\hat{g} \equiv g - (1-\alpha)t_w$$

that part of government expenditure financed from the capital share of income.

Theorem 3.1. A steady-state distribution exists for k .

The proof is analogous to that of Theorem 2.1.

The equation of motion for the price level is given by

(3.14)

$$\frac{dp}{p} = \left\{\left[\frac{1}{m}(\hat{g} - t_c\alpha) - (\alpha - \hat{g})\right]k^{\alpha-1} + c(1+m) + (1 - g')\left[(1 - g') - \frac{1}{m}(g' - t')\right]\sigma^2\right\}dt$$

$$+ \left[(1 - g') - \frac{1}{m}(g' - t')\right]\sigma dz \ .$$

Note from the deterministic part of (3.14) that an increase in the demand for money at a given capital-labor ratio is not guaranteed to reduce the expected rate of inflation. While a larger share of savings is allocated toward holdings of real money balances the consequence of the resulting increase in the value of outstanding debt is less overall savings.

It is more convenient to treat the rate of inflation as a policy parameter than the tax rates t_c and t' . The following two assumptions describe the postulated finance policy:

<u>Assumption 3.12</u>. The tax rate on the stochastic component is set at a level such that the stochastic component of the rate of inflation is zero.

It is assumed that money provides a momentarily safe return. This assumption implies that

(3.15) $$1 - t' = (1+m)(1 - g') \ .$$

<u>Assumption 3.13</u>. The tax rate on the deterministic component of income is set at a level such that the deterministic component of the rate of inflation is $\pi(k)$.

This assumption implies that

(3.16) $$1 - t_c(k) = (1+m)(1 - \hat{g}/\alpha) + \frac{m}{\alpha}[\pi(k) - c(1+m)]k^{1-\alpha} \ .$$

A function $\pi(k)$ is said to constitute an inflation policy.

The after-tax rate of return on capital is given by

$$(3.17) \qquad r_K dt + \sigma_K dz = \alpha(1 - t_c)k^{\alpha-1}dt - (1 - t')\sigma dz$$
$$= [(1+m)(\alpha-\hat{g})k^{\alpha-1} + m\pi(k) - mc(1+m)]dt - (m+1)(1 - g')\sigma dz.$$

It is assumed that the wealth holding class chooses its level of consumption and share of wealth held as real cash balances to maximize expected discounted utility of consumption over an infinite horizon. Their utility function is characterized by constant relative risk aversion

$$(3.18) \qquad u(c(t)) = e^{-\delta t}\frac{1}{\gamma}c^{\gamma}, \quad \gamma < 1, \quad \delta > 0 .$$

Each agent is small in that he considers his own savings and portfolio behavior not to affect the rates of return on capital and money. Finally, wealth holders are myopic in that they ignore the effect of changes in the capital-labor ratio on the rate of return on capital and inflation rate: they expect the mean rate of return on each asset to remain constant.[3] The negative of the inflation rate thus becomes the safe rate of return for the economy.

Merton [1969] shows that an optimizing consumer with utility function of the form (3.18) will choose consumption

$$(3.19) \qquad C^*(t) = \frac{\delta + \gamma[\pi - (r_K + \pi)^2/2(1-\gamma)\sigma_K^2]}{1 - \gamma} W(t)$$

---

[3] This last assumption is a serious restriction and a departure from the assumption of rational behavior. To relax it, however, is to invite intractability. See Merton [1973] for a further discussion of the problem.

and hold the risky asset in amount

$$(3.20) \qquad K(t) = \frac{r_K + \pi}{(1-\gamma)\sigma_K^2} W(t)$$

assuming that the transversality conditions of the consequent dynamic program are satisfied. These are satisfied here when $\gamma \leq 0$ and $\delta > 0$ or when $\gamma < 1$ and

$$\delta > \gamma \left[-\pi + \frac{(r_K + \pi)^2 (2-\gamma)}{2\sigma_K^2 (1-\gamma)} \right] .$$

The demand for money is

$$(3.21) \qquad M(t) = \left[1 - \frac{r_K + \pi}{(1-\gamma)\sigma_K^2} \right] W(t) .$$

It is assumed that the inflation policy is set to maintain a positive demand for money for all values of k . This implies

$$(3.22) \qquad r_K + \pi < (1-\gamma)\sigma_K^2 .$$

Substituting the expression for the rate of return on capital, (3.17) into expressions (3.19) and (3.20) yields as reduced form expressions for the consumption coefficient

$$(3.23) \qquad c = \frac{\delta + \gamma\pi}{1-\gamma} - \frac{\gamma(1 - g')^2 \sigma^2}{2}$$

and the demand for money coefficient

$$(3.24) \qquad m = \frac{1}{c}[(\alpha-\hat{g})k^{\alpha-1} + \pi - (1-g')(1-\gamma)\sigma^2] .$$

The positive relationship between desired money balances and the rate of inflation and the negative relationship between the demand for money and the variance term is surprising. Note from expression (3.17), however, that the variance of the rate of return on capital is an increasing function of the desired ratio of real money balances to capital. For this reason any value of m is compatible with a given level of $(1-g')\sigma^2$ and $(r_K + \pi)$.

At a given capital-labor ratio the rate of inflation is itself an increasing function of the demand for money. It is this relationship that is captured in expression (3.24).

Substituting the reduced form expressions for the consumption coefficient c and the desired ratio of real money balances to capital m into the equation of motion for the capital-labor ratio, (3.14) gives

$$(3.25) \qquad dk = \left[\frac{1}{2}(1-g')^2\sigma^2(2-\gamma) - (\pi(k) + \delta)/(1-\gamma) - n\right]kdt - (1-g')\sigma k dz .$$

Observe that a constant inflation policy $\pi(k) = \bar{\pi}$ implies that the capital-labor ratio is a random variable with log-normal distribution for which no steady-state distribution on $(0,\infty)$ exists.

The proof of Theorems 1 and 2 implies that if the inflation policy is of the form

$$(3.27) \qquad \pi(k) = -dk^{v-1} + e \ ; \quad 0 < v < 1 , \quad d > 0$$

and if

$$(3.28) \qquad n + \frac{\delta + e}{1-\gamma} - \frac{1}{2}(2-\gamma)(1-g')^2\sigma^2 > 0$$

then a steady-state distribution exists for k .

From the expression for the ratio of desired real money balances to capital, (3.24), a non-negative demand for money at all positive levels of the capital-labor ratio implies that

$$(3.29) \qquad v = \alpha$$

and

$$d < \alpha - \hat{g} \, .$$

Applying (A.9) to the stochastic differential equation (3.26), substituting condition (3.29), gives

$$(3.30) \qquad E[k^{\gamma-1}] = \frac{n + (\delta + e)/(1-\gamma) - \frac{1}{2}(1-\gamma)(1-g')^2\sigma^2}{d} \, .$$

The expected output-capital ratio is an increasing function of the rate of population growth, the discount rate and the parameters $-d$ and e . It is a decreasing function of $(1-g')^2\sigma^2$. In contrast with the result obtained in the case of fixed savings and portfolio behavior increased uncertainty in the underlying production relationship diminishes rather than augments the output-capital ratio. Furthermore, the output-capital ratio is an increasing function of the rate of inflation since the value of expression (3.30) is positively associated with the parameters e and $-d$.

Expressions (3.23), (3.24) and (3.30) characterize the fixed point or the general equilibrium of a dynamic stochastic economy. The propensity to consume, the demand for money and the expected output-capital ratio are related to parameters of the utility function, the production function and policy. Changes in these parameters affect the equilibrium through income effects, wealth effects and through their effects on the riskiness of capital and portfolio equilibrium. In the presence of all these it is difficult to identify the source of particular relationships.

The assumptions of this model are too special to cause one to discard the findings of Section II on the basis of this analysis. This model has demonstrated, however, that when the mode of government finance affects the relative riskiness as well as the mean rates of return on alternative assets and when wealth influences consumption the effects of alternative policies may differ radically from those suggested by the standard model.

APPENDIX

STEADY-STATE PROPERTIES OF DIFFUSION PROCESSES

This appendix presents a set of results on the properties of continuous-time diffusion processes used in Section II. It relies heavily on results due to Feller [1952], Mandl [1968], Bourgignon [1974], and Merton [1975].

In general a system of differential equations of the Itô type may be expressed as

$$\text{(A.1)} \qquad dy(t) = b(y(t))dt + a^{1/2}(y(t))dw(t)$$

where $y(t)$ is an n-vector of random variables, b is an n-vector of functions, a is an $n\times n$ matrix of functions and $dw(t)$ is an n-dimensional vector of independent Wiener processes.

The transition probability is defined as

$$\text{(A.2)} \qquad P(\bar{y}, t, y_0, t_0) = \Pr[y(t) \leq \bar{y} \mid y(t_0) = y_0] \ .$$

The forward Kolmogorov or Fokker-Planck equation, derived for the multidimensional case by Cox and Miller [1968] and Soong [1973], is the equation of motion of the probability density function (p.d.f.) corresponding to (A.2). It is given by the partial differential equation

$$\text{(A.3)} \qquad \frac{\partial p(y, t, y_0, t_0)}{\partial t} = \sum_{i=1}^{n} \frac{\partial b_i(y)p(y, t, y_0, t_0)}{\partial y_i} + \frac{1}{2} \sum_{i,j=1}^{n} \frac{\partial^2 a_{ij}(y)p(y, t, y_0, t_0)}{\partial y_i \partial y_j} \ .$$

When expression (A.3) is equal to zero the transition probability is stationary.

The stationary joint-probability function $p(y_1, \ldots, y_n)$ is given by the solution of the partial differential equation obtained by setting expression (A.3) equal to zero. Solutions have not been found for the general multi-dimensional case. For the case $n = 1$ the solution is given by

$$\text{(A.4)} \qquad p(y) = m_1 a^{-1}(y)\exp c(y) + m_2 a^{-1}(y)\exp c(y)\int^y \exp(-2c(z))dz$$

where

$$c(y) = 2\int^y \frac{b(u)}{a(u)}\,du \ .$$

The constants m_1 and m_2 aré set so that

$$\text{(A.5)} \qquad \int_{-\infty}^{\infty} p(y)dy = 1 \ .$$

Theorems by Feller [1952] and Mandl [1968] demonstrate that a non-trivial stationary distribution for a diffusion process of the form (A.1) exists if and only if all absorbing boundaries are inaccessible. A point b is defined as an absorbing boundary of the process (A.1) when

$$\text{(A.6)} \qquad P(b, t, y, t_0) = 1 \text{ and}$$

$$P(y, t, y, t_0) = 0 \ , \quad y < b \quad \forall t > t_1$$

where t_1 is the first-passage time to b. The boundary b is accessible if $E(t_1) < \infty$ and inaccessible otherwise.

A theorem due to Bourgignon [1974] based on results of Feller [1952] and Mandl [1968, p. 92] states the following conditions as necessary and sufficient for the existence of a one-dimensional diffusion process with absorbing boundaries b_1 and b_2

(A.7a) $\exp[-c(y)] \notin I(b_i, y_0)$, $i = 1, 2$

(A.7b) $a^{-1}(y)\exp[c(y)] \in I(b_i, y_0)$, $i = 1, 2$

where $I(a,b)$ is the family of functions integrable on $[a,b]$. Condition (A.7a) implies that the second term of (A.4) is unbounded, implying that if $p(y)$ is a true p.d.f. then $m_2 = 0$.

A heuristic interpretation of these conditions is that, in the neighborhood of an absorbing barrier b_i , the drift term of the diffusion process $b(y)$ be large relative to the variance term $a(y)$ and have a sign such that it is repelled from the boundary.

The expected value of certain functions of y in steady-state may be calculated without an explicit solution for its asymptotic p.d.f. as long as the conditions for the existence of a non-trivial p.d.f. are satisfied. Soong [1973, pp. 202-203] shows that, for any function $h(y,t)$ jointly continuous and bounded on any finite interval:

$$\text{(A.8)} \qquad \frac{dE[h(y,t)]}{dt} = \sum_{i=1}^{n} E[b_i(y)h_i] + \frac{1}{2}\sum_{i,j=1}^{n} E[a_{ij}(y)h_{ij}] + E[h_t]$$

where $h_t = \partial h(y,t)/\partial t$, $h_i = \partial h(y,t)/\partial y_i$, and $h_{ij} = \partial^2 h/\partial y_i \partial y_j$. If $h(y,t)$ is stationary then $h(y,t) = h(y)$. If, furthermore, y is stationary then

$$\frac{dE[h(y)]}{dt} = E[h_t] = 0 \ .$$

This implies

$$\text{(A.9)} \qquad \sum_{i=1}^{n} E[b_i(y)h_i] + \sum_{i,j=1}^{n} [a_{ij}(y)h_{ij}] = 0 \ .$$

REFERENCES

Blinder, A. S. and R. M. Solow [1973]. "Does Fiscal Policy Matter?" Journal of Public Economics, 2, pp. 319-337.

Bourgignon, F. [1974]. "A Particular Class of Continuous-Time Stochastic Growth Models," Journal of Economic Theory, 9, pp. 141-158.

Brock, W. A. and L. J. Mirman [1972]. "Optimal Economic Growth and Uncertainty: The Discounted Case," Journal of Economic Theory, 4, pp. 479-513.

Cox, D. A. and H. D. Miller [1968]. The Theory of Stochastic Processes. New York: John Wiley and Sons.

Feldstein, M. [1975]. "Inflation, Income Taxes and the Rate of Interest: A Theoretical Analysis," Discussion Paper Number 414, Harvard Institute of Economic Research (May).

Feller, W. [1952]. "The Parabolic Differential Equation and the Associated Semi-Group of Transformations," Mathematical Analysis.

_________ [1968]. An Introduction to Probability Theory and Its Applications, 3rd edition. New York: John Wiley and Sons.

Foley, D. K. and M. Sidrauski [1971]. Monetary and Fiscal Policy in a Growing Economy. London: Macmillan Company.

Green, J. and E. Sheshinsky [1975]. Budget Displacement Effects of Inflationary Finance. Technical Report No. 180, Institute for Mathematical Studies in the Social Sciences, Stanford University (Sept.).

Mandl, P. [1968]. Analytical Treatment of One-Dimensional Markov Processes. Prague: Academia.

Merton, R. C. [1969]. "Lifetime Portfolio Selection Under Uncertainty: The Continuous-Time Case," Review of Economics and Statistics, 51, pp. 247-257.

_________ [1973]. "An Intertemporal Capital Asset Pricing Model," Econometrica, 41, pp. 867-887.

_________ [1975]. "An Asymptotic Theory of Growth under Uncertainty," Review of Economic Studies, 42(3), pp. 375-394.

Mirman, L. J. [1973]. "The Steady State Behavior of a Class of One Sector Growth Models with Uncertain Technology," Journal of Economic Theory, 6, pp. 219-242.

Mirrlees, J. A. [1971]. "Optimum Growth and Uncertainty," Unpublished paper presented at the I.E.A. Workshop in Economic Theory, Bergen.

Soong, T. T. [1973]. Random Differential Equations in Science and Engineering. New York: Academic Press.

Solow, R. M. [1970]. Growth Theory. New York: Oxford University Press.

Tobin, J. [1958]. "Liquidity Preference as Behavior Toward Risk," Review of Economic Studies, 25, pp. 65-86.

________ [1966]. "Money and Economic Growth," Econometrica, 33, pp. 671-684.

________ and W. Buiter [1975]. "Long Run Effects of Fiscal and Monetary Policy on Aggregate Demand," Proceedings of the Conference on Monetarism, edited by J. Stein. Amsterdam: North-Holland, forthcoming.